GOD'S LAST WORD

Are we ready?

JOHN J WEATHERHOGG

GOD'S LAST WORD

Are we ready?

MEMOIRS
Cirencester

Published by Memoirs

MEMOIRS
PUBLISHING

1A The Market Place Cirencester, Gloucestershire, GL7 2PR
info@memoirsbooks.co.uk   www.memoirspublishing.com

ISBN 978-1-86151-060-0

Printed in England

List of Contents

FOREWORD

It has been my privilege to know Dr John Weatherhogg for many years, not only as a respected Bible teacher, but also as a dear friend and fellow-worker. Those who know him well have appreciated his keen interest in eschatology especially the doctrine of the Second Advent. As he indicates in this book, his interest in this subject was acquired during his formative years as a Christian, and is closely linked to his own personal experience of war time Britain. Like so many of his generation, that harrowing experience, has been indelibly etched on his life, and has undoubtedly enhanced his writings on this important prophetic subject. Over the years he has contributed a number of impressive articles to the Prophetic Witness Magazine, and his first book, published in 2008, provides a comprehensive survey of all those prophetic events that will one day culminate in the Second Advent of Christ.

His second book, a commentary on the last book of the New Testament, is a genuine attempt on his part to let the Bible speak for itself. Of the writing of commentaries on Revelation there is no end so why do we think that John's short commentary will be a useful addition? There are two main reasons:

The first is that it is rare in this modern age to find anyone writing a commentary on a biblical text who has not thoroughly engaged critically with other writers in the same field. It is not, however, unprecedented, as inner-biblical interpretation has historically been a tried and tested approach to biblical exegesis. Put simply, the interpretation of the Bible actually begins within the Bible itself. Anyone reading biblical narrative will immediately sense that the writers of these sacred texts are constantly interacting with each other in the revelation of divine truth. This internal dialogue remains vitally important if we are to clearly understand God's ultimate purposes in the person and work of Jesus Christ. To this end, John has written this helpful commentary on Revelation so that we might be principally guided by Scripture to correctly interpret God's last word to men. Or in the words of another writer on prophecy of an earlier age, S. P. Tregelles, "Remarks' are so connected with the portions of Scripture to which they relate, that, for them to be rightly followed, the Bible should be kept open for continual reference".

The second is that most commentaries written on this important New Testament text have a tendency either to over complicate issues or are far too technical in nature for the ordinary reader. One could, of course, argue that this is a reflection of the book itself, hence the reason why so many Christians find the book almost impenetrable. John's unpretentious approach, however, not only enables the ordinary reader to grasp the significance of profound future events, but even more advanced students will value the perspicuity of his comments and his considerable understanding of divine truth.

Not everyone who reads this book will necessary agree with John's dispensational position or his view that only the 'Futurist' viewpoint per se is relevant to the interpretation of the book. Others have argued in the past that there is some grain of truth in all four hermeneutic viewpoints, but what predominates is the aspect of unfulfilled prophecy, which is the thrust of the 'Futurist' viewpoint. Be that as it may though, John's arguments throughout this book are arrived at by a clear process of scriptural referrals, and where he is unsure of his ground, it is typical of him to acknowledge his limitations.

This book has been written during a period of great personal difficulty for John so in that sense he is totally able to empathize with his name-sake the Apostle John in his literary task. Our prayer is that this book will be of great help to God's people in their understanding of the book of Revelation.

'Even so, come Lord Jesus'.

Brian Clatworthy,
Bradley Evangelical Church,
Newton Abbot,
2013.

ACKNOWLEDGEMENTS.

As some of you will already know that in 2008 I published a book entitled, "What is the World coming to?" Also between 1995 and 2003, I wrote a number of articles which were published in "Prophetic Witness". I had also aimed at producing a further book but a mixture of health and age, both of myself and also of that of my wife steadily slowed down this proposal. However, in the year 2010, I felt that the Lord was telling me that this was the right time to commence a new book. Any further delay will lead to a total loss of the considerable time already spent on this work.

Looking back to my earlier work, I do thank God for the willingness of the editor Glyn Taylor in accepting a totally unknown writer in my early days. I would also thank Colin Le Noury for his guidance and encouragement. I would also thank Alec Passmore who encouraged me to write my original book. His enthusiasm was the main factor in confirming that I should continue writing regularly. I have appreciated his encouragement and friendship since then. My sincere thanks for the excellent assistance given to me by my friend Brian Clatworthy, who is one of the few that I can trust to present God's message in all of its glory.

My last thanks have been reserved for my family without whose help my task would have been considerably more difficult and the script less readable. It is with joy that I thank God for the all the help given to me in this venture by my wife Sylvia, my daughter Deborah and my two sons Nick and Tim. They have all been faithful in proof-reading, suggesting various corrections and when necessary giving me honest criticism. Finally, I must record my sincere thanks and appreciation for all the loving encouragement and support that Sylvia has given to me during the many months of research, writing and re-writing necessary for this work. Without her love and unwavering reassurance this work may never have been completed. This is despite the fact that she is totally blind in one eye and almost blind in the other. We cannot always understand why this should happen but we do pray and trust that the Lord will heal her soon.

An additional problem has also caused further delays as I have been diagnosed with Alzheimer's. I had hoped that I would be able to complete my book much earlier than this, but I must learn to trust. Finally, there was also the problem of some minor errors caused by punctuation, spelling, etc. My daughter, Deborah, has been excellent in helping me to sort out these various items. Without her help there is much that would have been lost.

J.J.W.

PERSONAL INTRODUCTION TO THE AUTHOR

For most of my working life I have been involved in various spheres of engineering commencing with an indentured apprenticeship. In 1947 I felt called to study for full-time Christian work, so I enrolled at the National Young Life Campaign Bible College. After completing the course I then spent the following year in evangelistic work, which I expected would lead to full-time Christian work. It was at that time that I met the young lady who later became my wife and we prayed together for guidance for our future. It became clear that the Lord was leading me back into industry, not merely to make that my career, but to be useful in Christian service in the many small places of worship without being a financial burden to them. I then returned to normal work but only one position was available. I felt that it was a retrograde step because it was low grade work. However, the Lord was in control and within a short space of time I was offered the opportunity of transferring to the tool design department where I eventually became a senior tool designer. I studied privately and obtained qualifications that led into a teaching career in a Technical College.

During this time the Lord gave me many blessings. In Christian Work He gave me increasing opportunities for systematic Bible ministry. I was also offered the post of Senior Lecturer in "Manufacturing Systems" in a large Polytechnic. Then later, I was given the opportunity of improving my qualifications and as a result obtained B.Sc.(Econ)., M.Sc.(Eng)., Ph.D. & D.I.C. all from the University of London. These qualifications were not for me to use for my own advantages, the Lord had given them to me for a purpose. For many years I have had a deep interest in the Second Coming of our Lord Jesus, and there is much that God has taught me through His servants and His Word. What I did not realise at the time, was that my academic studies which covered a wide range of subjects such as industrial economics, labour control, political control and influences over industry, have given me an important background into many of the problems and situations prevalent today. They have helped me understand many of the Prophesies concerned with the situations nowadays.

After much prayer concerning the subject I should choose, I was drawn to the wonderful book of Revelation. Many would consider this book to be difficult to understand, but I discovered that the more I read it, the more I believe the Holy Spirit guided my way and revealed to me that this special Book had much to teach us. The more that I read this Book, the more I am convinced that this has much more to reveal to us. I have spent much time reading Revelation over the past two and half years. This is a special Book, quite different from every other portion of Scripture. I also believe that the Lord was challenging me to study His word rather than what others had written concerning what they believed was the correct interpretation. Because of this there are only a few references listed from other parts of the Scriptures and also few from the work of others, many of whom have done excellent work for the Lord.

I close with another reminder of how good God is. My wife and I celebrated our Diamond Wedding in 2012 when we reminded ourselves of God's guidance, love and protection over sixty years of marriage. An additional blessing is that our daughter and two sons together with their two wives have each committed their lives to the Lord Jesus, so we are a family united in His love.

J.J.W.

AN INTRODUCTION TO THE SITUATION TODAY OBVIOUSLY SETS THE PATERN FOR THE FUTURE EVENTS RECORDED IN THE BOOK OF THE REVELATION OF JESUS CHRIST.

Almost the entire book of Revelation is concerned with the future, so before we commence this study we need to review briefly the importance of the main events which we see around us today. I believe that this will lead to a better understanding of this special Book.

History will also show that by far the majority of great civilisations have developed from the area around the Mediterranean Sea and the "Middle East". Although there were other great civilisations such as China and the Incas of South America, none of these compared with the vast control achieved by the four kingdoms mentioned in the Book of Daniel. Compared with other great civilisations, these four kingdoms are unique. God has chosen these as the foundation for His plan that will ultimately be the fulfilment of many prophecies which He has given us.

A study of scripture and history will reveal that in the past there were four powerful nations that controlled the known world of that time. The first of these was Babylon (c 606 BC), next was Media-Persia (c 530 BC), then there was Greece (c 331 BC) and finally there was Rome (68 BC – 476 AD). As we all know, our Lord left Heaven and was born on this earth and was crucified by Roman soldiers. Many of the saints of that era were also crucified. The influence of Rome both past and present has influenced many nations. Rome appeared to be benevolent at the start of its world control, but gradually became supremely powerful. Eventually many of the Caesars claimed equality with the multitude of their gods and demanded worship from their subjects. Since the fall of the Roman Empire there has never been another total world power, although many have attempted it. These include Charlemagne, Napoleon, Bismark, Hitler, Stalin and many others. However, there is coming a day when there will be one supreme dictator who will control the entire population of all who live on this earth. This will be the Antichrist who will usurp total power and authority over the whole world for just a short period of time.

Over the past few years there has been a steady change concerning the relationship between almost all nations. Two obvious examples are the rise of the E.U. together with the rise of Islam. In addition to this there are apparent changes to the aims of many powerful countries such as the U.S.A., Russia and China. Some have attempted to control other nations by agreeing to various treaties, some have enforced new laws upon others, and some have used the control of money and banking systems. One of the most important aspects which show us the urgency of these present days is the situation concerning the reduction in the number of faithful churches which are still preaching the true gospel. The author of this book can clearly remember the true Christian outreach which was the norm for Sunday services both before the last war, throughout that time and for a few years afterwards. An example of the Christian outreach in those days soon after the war ended was that one evangelist preached regularly in a crowded Royal Albert Hall on a Saturday evening every month. It was a strait forward service with no gimmicks and many were converted. Another amazing situation was that the gospel was preached faithfully in a crowded Westminster Abbey by a nonconformist evangelist and an evangelical Anglican. These examples were typical of how God blessed our country at that time. More recently, there has been a complete reversal of this situation. Many of our churches and chapels have been closed permanently, many have been changed into shops, homes and other buildings, and there are also those who have even been taken over by false religions.

This should not surprise us if we understand the teaching of Scripture. When God's special people turned their back upon Him, He warned them in very clear terms of the severe results of backsliding. This warning is given many times throughout scripture in both the Old and the New Testaments.

A Personal Note.

For many years, I have had a strong desire to make a study of this wonderful book and in addition to this I have also believed that it was right for me to approach this study with only a minimum of references to any commentaries. The more often that I read this tremendous book, the more that I understood that there was much that God had already revealed to us that leads us to an understanding of His Word. Obviously over the years of reading God's word and also of listening to many faithful servants expounding God's messages, I have imbibed much that was challenging and encouraging. My reason for stating this is that I have endeavoured to study this important book by using only what God has given to us in His Word. In analysing this Book, one of the most important aspects is the continual emphasis upon the location of each event. There are three main locations and these are Heaven, Earth and Hell. By understanding this, the development of the majority of each event is readily appreciated.

God's severe warning concerning the last days.

"Behold the days are coming," says the Lord God, "That I will send a famine on the land, not a famine of bread, nor a thirst for water, but of hearing the words of the Lord. They shall wander from sea to sea and from north to east; they shall run to and fro seeking the word of the Lord but will not find it". Amos 8:11-12.

"They shall go and seek the Lord but they will not find Him because He has withdrawn Himself from them". Hosea 5:6.

"If we sin wilfully after we have received a knowledge of the truth, there no longer remains a sacrifice for sins, but a certain fearful expectation of judgement". Hebrews 10:26-27.

A REVIEW OF THE PRE-MILLENNIAL, PRE-TRIBULATION RETURN OF THE LORD JESUS CHRIST AS TAUGHT CLEARLY IN THE BOOK OF REVELATION.

In many ways the Book of Revelation is undoubtedly one of the most difficult to understand; therefore there is a great tendency for many to avoid all but a few passages which are more easily understood. For many it has been a neglected book and we need to remedy this now and to spend time studying it, learning from it and enjoying God's word. We need to know this book, to love it and to apply its lessons to ourselves. We must never however expect to understand it unless we are willing to spend considerable time allowing the Holy Spirit to reveal God's Word to us. The more we read and study Revelation, the more we realise how little we really understand it and how much more there is to comprehend. The majority of the references from the Book of Revelation are given only in terms of chapter and verse.

A. SETTING THE BASIS FOR OUR STUDY.

1. An introduction to our study.

My first real interest in the Doctrine of the Second Coming was as a young teenager when I attended a tent mission in the greater London area. This commenced over the last few days of August and continued for the first few days of September in 1939. As you will readily see, the daily news created much interest for these services. As a result of the new situation, the tent had to be abandoned (because of the new regulations concerning the blackout) and the services continued in a large local church. At that time, there was much in prophecy that we were unable to appreciate. The background of prophetic history of the nations has changed much since then and the overall facts of the Second Coming have become much clearer. We must, however, beware of reading into prophecy our own ideas, what we believe might happen in the future. It is probably impossible to come to this study without some preconceived theories. For many of us, these are the results of all the teaching and influences that we have imbibed over many years of Christian experience. Much of this will be of great help, but we do need to have that wisdom from God to understand what is the true interpretation of Scripture and not merely something that appears to "fit in" with our own interpretation. We need to pray sincerely for wisdom in order to understand what God would teach us.

2. **Revelation has a unique place in Scripture and there are four essential reasons why this is so:**

(a) The promise that "Blessed is he that reads ... that hears ... that keeps (takes to heart N.I.V.) ... the things that are written", 1:3.

(b) These are the very last Words which God has given us and as such they are of vital importance to an understanding of the future.

(c) They also include the severe warning, "Do not add ... do not take away", 22:18-19. This warning must be heeded as it is so easy to add our own ideas and interpretations to God's word. Just as serious is it to tone down or even to remove some aspect of God's Revelation. Just because some portions of scripture are not obvious or they may even appear to be incorrect when viewed from the purely human point of view, gives us no authority to alter or ignore any of God's Holy word.

(d) There are many difficult passages in Revelation and we must avoid introducing our own concepts, therefore we need to pray for the gift of "Spiritual discernment" in order to understand what we read.

3. **What criteria should we apply to a study of the Book of Revelation?**

(a) It is well known by most Bible students that there are four distinct interpretations concerning the teaching of the

Second Coming. In addition, each one of these may have additional minor variations emphasising some aspect. Personally I believe that the "Pre-rapture, Pre-millennium" teaching gives a much better understanding of the Second Coming than the other three interpretations. This is often referred to as "Dispensational Pre-millennialism". I trust that our study of Revelation will confirm this interpretation.

(b) In addition to this, there are four clear viewpoints each of which seeks to interpret the order of events in Revelation.

(i) **The Preterite viewpoint.** This states that the whole book was written only for John's time and its meanings were obvious to those at that time which is why it is difficult to understand now. In reality the opposite is true. The details given concerning these events are such that in John's time they would have little or no application. This viewpoint also ignores the vital statement that states clearly, "I will show you what must take place after this", 4:1, which then gives a systematic unfolding of many events most of them still in the future.

(ii) **The Futurist viewpoint** which I believe gives a clear indication of God's plan for the future. Chapters 2 and 3 are considered to be the historical development of the Church from Pentecost to the Rapture. There is then a clear break between 3:22 and 4:1, which is indicated by the phrase "After these things", 4:1. From this point onwards all the teaching is concerned entirely with the future. Throughout the rest of this book there is a constant emphasis upon the development of the next series of God's great plan of events. This I believe gives a clear insight into an understanding of the teaching of Revelation.

(iii) **The Historical viewpoint.** The whole book is considered to be a gradual unfolding of God's plan for His Church throughout the ages. A careful review of this interpretation will reveal that this ignores the fact that it is only chapters 2 and 3 that are concerned with past history. A study of chapter 5:9 will reveal that those who have been redeemed will now be in Heaven.

(iv) **The Idealist viewpoint.** This views Revelation as concerned almost entirely with Christian experience and although there is much teaching of this important subject, even a superficial examination will show that this is an unfolding of God's plan for the future. John is told, "Write ... what will take place later", 1:19, and "I will show you what must take place after this", 4:1. Chapters 4 to 22 are concerned mainly with events which are still in the future and any challenge to a more Godly life is based on an understanding of the implications of those coming events.

4. The essential requirements when reviewing prophesy.

(a) We must approach Scripture in humility and with a willingness to be guided by the Holy Spirit and if necessary to abandon our own preconceived ideas.

(b) No interpretation may contradict the basic teaching of Scripture. The book of Revelation may enlighten or add further details to other Scriptures but it will never contradict them.

(c) We must compare the similarities with all the other prophecies both within the New Testament as well as those in the Old Testament such as those of Daniel, Zechariah and Ezekiel.

5. Prophecy is often not understood until a short period of time before its fulfilment.

For example, Daniel was unable to understand the meaning of some of those prophecies that he had been given. He was told quite clearly that they were "sealed till the last days", Dan 12:1-13. See particularly v9. The Book of the Revelation is especially a description of the last days. Therefore as we believe that we are living in those last days now, most of the prophecies in Revelation should become clearer as we approach their fulfilment. Three examples illustrate this point:

(a) "Hail and fire mingled with blood, and they were cast upon the earth: and the third part of trees was burnt up ... and all green grass burnt up, and the third part of the creatures in the sea died; and the third part of the ships were destroyed ... The third part of the waters became wormwood (bitter) and many men died of the waters ... A third of the sun, the moon and the stars were also struck." 8:7-12.   This describes very accurately what could probably be the result of a nuclear war together with nuclear fallout. We must never be too dogmatic about our own interpretation as modern warfare often changes the situation rapidly. There may still be many more surprises yet to come. These prophecies are amazing when we bear in mind that John had no knowledge of any modern warfare yet some of his special visions are understood clearly today.

(b) "The fourth angel poured out his vial upon the sun: and power was given unto (the sun) to scorch men with fire. And men were scorched with great heat ... the earth was full of darkness and they gnawed their tongues because of the pain", 16:8-11. This could describe nuclear fallout, or the breakup of the ozone layer either of which could produce terrible cancerous devastation amongst humans. Until Hiroshima with its ghastly results and the more recent problems of the ozone layer, this prophecy was meaningless.

(c) The drying up of the Euphrates, 16:12. Today, Turkey has dammed the river Euphrates to obtain water and there is already a likelihood of it drying up in Iraq (Babylon).

These three possible situations may be understood for the first time ever, but we must also appreciate that modern claims of science are changing rapidly and any interpretation may vary considerably from time to time. In addition to this we cannot always understand what God has revealed in His prophecies, so we must be very careful how we interpret any future events.

6. **There are very important differences between Revelation and many other prophecies.**

All the other prophecies are based almost entirely upon the fact that "The Lord **SAID**", whereas much of Revelation (after chapter 3) is based upon what John **SAW**. John wrote what he saw, although he may not have understood what God had revealed to him. However, guided by the Holy Spirit he portrayed it in such detail that we can appreciate it today, although we may not at this stage understand it completely. Another important aspect is that these prophecies are quite different from the many prophecies listed in the Old Testament where the fulfilment was often within the life of the prophet or shortly afterwards. The prophecies in our studies were given around two thousand years ago and are still awaiting fulfilment. Since then, the world and all the systems concerned with mankind have changed radically, yet we can understand much of what God has revealed to us through His Word.

Many of John's visions were not understood until our recent knowledge of modern warfare and even then we still have much more to understand.

He describes what he sees but his knowledge is very limited indeed and we are left to understand them in the light of present day events. In Dan 12:4 we read, "Seal up the book to the time of the end". This was because the visions cannot be understood until that time "of the end". Perhaps it is possible that the Lord God (Who created time) permitted John to move forward in time and actually see what would happen in the last days. Some of the visions are so accurate that we can now understand many of the aspects of these prophecies that were not appreciated until recently. Other prophecies may still be veiled to us until God reveals them to us in His time.

The application of symbolism is also very important and must be compared with the symbolism used throughout scripture. This especially applies to some sections in books such as Daniel, Ezekiel and Zechariah.

7. John is mainly concerned with the results of the judgements rather than with the means used to produce them.

Two causes of severe destruction are present throughout chapters 6 to 19 and the first of these is that for a limited period God will withdraw His restraining Hand from the earth and permit Satan and his followers to have a limited control of the earth. The second cause of severe disasters will be that God Himself will pour out His Judgements upon mankind. It is highly likely that the Lord God will create new means of destruction and if so this may account for the difficulty in understanding some passages. Many of the judgements could be caused by natural phenomena such as earthquakes, floods, drought, storms or plagues but far worse than any experienced previously. These will be brought about either by God's direct intervention or as the result of man's greed and sinfulness. Further disasters could be caused by nuclear or chemical warfare whilst further devastation may be the result of demon activity. As the final disasters will include a whole range of terrible events, the Tribulation and the Battle of Armageddon will be far worse than anything known throughout history. We must avoid attempting to "spiritualise" any passage unless there is a good reason for doing so.

8   The importance of the order of events.

Unless there is any reason to believe otherwise, we must consider the events in Revelation to be in a reasonable chronological order. However we must not expect a totally rigid order of events. God does not always do things in the same way that we would.   An analysis of Revelation chapters 4 to 22 will demonstrate this fact quite clearly. This is seen by the continual repetition of the following phrases together with others that the reader will discover as they study this wonderful book.

In Chapters 4:1, 7:1 & 9, 18:1, 19:1, 21:1 we see very clearly the steady progress of some future events: "I will show you things which must take place **after this**". In chapters 8, 9, 10 & 11 there is a similar repetition of "**then**". There is also the repetition of the seven events such as; "when He opened the second seal" ... etc. ...and also "when He opened the seventh seal" in chapter 6:1-17 and chapter 8:1. See also the same increment for the seven trumpets (in chapters 8 & 9), and also for the bowls full of the wrath of God (in chapters 15 & 16).

All of this demonstrates clearly a pattern of steady development throughout much of the book of Revelation.

However there are a few passages which may produce a difficulty in deciding whether or not they present an exact order of events. Some believe that these are two versions of the same event, others believe that the trumpets are warnings of "wrath to come" and the bowls being the actual punishments. In addition there are those who believe that they are similar judgements but with increasing intensity. This situation is noted when comparing the seven trumpets and the seven bowls of the Wrath of God. There is no real problem and no sign of any contradiction throughout this book. We must always remind ourselves that God has stated that, "For as the heavens are higher than the earth, so are my ways higher than your ways, and My thoughts higher than your thoughts", Isaiah 55:9.

There are also a few passages which may be considered as "flashbacks" to earlier events in order to emphasise a point such as "chapter 12". This is God's special book which is His absolute final message to a world that has rejected Him. We must not therefore expect all that He teaches us will be obvious and easy to understand. There may be some sections which we will never fully understand until we see Him face to face in eternity.

9.   The emphasis upon the Holy Spirit.

The Holy Spirit is often referred to as "The Spirit" see: 1:10, 2:7, 2:11, 2:17, 2:29, 3:6, 3:13, 3:22, 4:2 & 14:13. Occasionally the title of "Holy" is omitted as in 21:10 & 22:17 but we must never use this to believe that He is not Holy.

There are a number of references which are given the title of "Seven Spirits". These have been chosen by God for special responsibilities. 1:4, 3:1, 4:5 and 5:6.

The false spirits that are referred to in 16:13, 16:14 and 18:2 are quite different from the "Holy Spirit". Satan often attempts to copy or to destroy the work of God. As we know, Satan is always defeated when he attempts this.

10. The Importance of the location and meaning of Heaven, Hell and the Earth in each Prophecy.

An appreciation of these three main locations will help us to understand the essential underlying teaching of God's plan for the final last days. The Book of Revelation lists the three main divisions of these locations. These are as follows:

(a) The term of "Heaven" is used for quite different locations as follows:

(i) The abode of Almighty God together with His angels and other special beings.

(ii) The term "Heaven" is also used for the abode of Satan. It is obvious that this has an entirely different meaning from that of above (i) but may also refer to (iii) or (iv).

(iii) The stars and our planetary system.

(iv) The atmosphere and the clouds, etc. around our earth.

(b) Our planet earth has a special relationship because of the fact that the Lord Jesus lived on this earth with mankind in order to bring salvation.

(c) Hell, Hades and Death are all names that are used for Hell see 1:18, 6:8, 20:13 & 14. The title of "Hell" does not occur in some versions of the scriptures.

(d) Closely connected to the teaching of Hell are those referring to the abode of Satan and his host of evil demons. This includes the bottomless pit in 17:8

11. The use of numbers throughout Revelation.

Much emphasis is placed upon the use of numbers especially that of seven. Although there is some symbolism in this, great care must be taken not to apply this to every situation.

Seven has an important application throughout the Book of Revelation. It is the number for perfection or completion and some of the essential usages for the value of seven are now listed. Only a few references at this stage are listed as others will be referred to as we progress with our studies. Some of the more important groups of sevens are now listed: Angels 11:15; Candlesticks 1:12; Churches 2 & 3; Heads 12:3, 13:1, 17:3 & 17:7; Kings 17:10; Mountains 17:9; Plagues 15:6; Seals 5:1 & 8:1; Spirits 4:5; Stars 1:16 & 1:20 & Thunders 10:4.

Some numbers are symbolic and some have a practical

application while others may combine both. The city distinguished as "seven mountains (or hills)" 17:9 is usually accepted to refer to the location depicting Rome.

The number 1000 is used six times in chapter twenty to refer to the special time span of the Millennium. This will therefore be dealt with later in our study.

Other numbers used in Revelation are as follows:

"One" 25 times.   "Two" 13 times.
"Three or a third" 33 times.   "Four or fourth" 36 times.
"Five or fifth" 22 times   "Six or sixth" 8 times.
"Ten" 11 times.   "Twelve" 21 times.
"Twenty" 29 times.

12. The Main Characters in the Book of Revelation.

The significance of each of these is essential to an understanding of the whole Book.

The obvious most important Persons are those of the Almighty Triune God and all those who have accepted His authority.

(a) The Triune God; God the Father, God the Son and God the Holy Spirit. There are only two alternatives. All will either be one with the true God or they will be allied with Satan as listed under below. There is no other alternative possible.

(b) There are important aspects of the Church throughout our studies. These are on earth in chap 1-3; in Heaven in chap 5; as the "Bride" of Christ in chap 19; in the Millennium Reign of Christ in chap 20; and finally "in the glory of the New Jerusalem" in chap 21 & 22.

(c) The twenty four Elders in chap 4:1 - 5:14 and 11:15-19. These are special saints that are usually considered to be the 12 Patriarchs and the 12 disciples.

(d) The Four Living creatures (beasts A.V.) 4:6-9. These are the special saints that are usually considered to be heavenly servants of God, sometimes associated with the twenty four Elders.

(e) The angels. These are God's Heavenly messengers and servants. There are also special angels who include the "Strong Angel", 5:2 and those with God's final message, chap 14.

(f) The 144,000 servants that are chosen from Israel to proclaim God's message during the Tribulation, chapter 7:14.

(g) The Tribulation Saints and Martyrs. Those refusing the Mark of the Beast, but rather accepting the Mark of the Lord, 7:1-17, 12:1-17 & 14:1-13. There are also parallels with the "144,000".

(h) The Woman in the Desert: Israel, chapter 12.

(i) The Two special servants of God who are probably Elijah and Moses, chapter 11.

Satan and all those allied with Him.

(a) Satan himself. He is referred to as the Dragon, the Great Red Dragon or the Great Dragon eight times in chap 12, three times in chap 13, and also in chap 16 and 20. He is also referred to as Satan seven times throughout the Book of Revelation and four times as the Serpent.

(b) The Antichrist. He is never called this in the K.J.V. or the N.K.J.V. of Revelation but may be in other versions. His main title is that of the "Beast" which occurs 44 times. This must never be confused with the "Four Beasts" who are also known as "The Four Living Creatures" in section 12 (d) above.

(c) The False Prophet. The Antichrist's chief deputy responsible for all religious control. The Beast out of the Earth, 13:11-18.

(d) The "whore" referred to as the "harlot" is riding on the Beast which is the Antichrist see (b) above. She is also referred to as Babylon the Great and the Apostate Church, chapter 17.

(e) Fallen Angels. The angel of the bottomless pit is named Abaddon or Apollyon, 9:11, and there also are four unnamed angels, 9:14-15.

(f) Demons and unclean spirits, 16:13-14 & 18:2.

(g) All those who through the ages have rejected the way of life offered by the Almighty Holy God.

(h) All those receiving the Mark of the Beast, 14:9-10.

13. Locations and their importance.

(a) Babylon, 17:18. Babel was the first systematic religious system to defy God and was the originator of the first system of Astrology and Occult Practices. History shows that this system was developed still further by Egypt, Assyria, Neo Babylon, Greece and Rome, whose systems were a mixture of political power, the occult, idolatry and the deification of their kings. They were all licentious, cruel, completely self-centred and utterly ruthless and were symbolic of the system to be set up by the Antichrist.

(b) Rome. Never mentioned by the actual name of "Rome" in the Book of Revelation, but referred to as the city upon the "seven mountains (or hills)", 17:9. Babylon and Rome were often used interchangeably by contemporary writers because Rome was the final culmination of the religious, political, social and military system initiated by Babylon. Peter in his Epistle uses Babylon as a synonym for Rome, 1 Peter 5:13.

(c) The River Euphrates, 9:14. Marks the traditional barrier between East and West. Prophecy makes it quite clear that It will be dried up to open the way for the "kings of the East" to attack the Antichrist, 16:12.

(d) Jerusalem. This historical city is mentioned only rarely, "The court (of the Temple) ... is to be given to the Gentiles and the Holy City (Jerusalem) they shall tread it under foot for forty two months", 11:2. This has parallels elsewhere in Scripture, Zech 14:2 & Luke 21:20-24. References to the "New Jerusalem" are all concerned with Christ's Kingdom, 3:12, 21:2 & 21:10.

(e) Armageddon (or Har-Magedon). Only mentioned in 16:16 and refers to the location of the final great battle although common usage usually refers to the battle itself. Often considered to be the "Mount of Megiddo". See 2 Kings 23:29, 2 Chron 35:22, Judges 5:19, plus others not in Scripture.

B. THE INTRODUCTION TO THE PROPHECY ITSELF.

1. The Purpose of this special Book. 1:1-3.

The purpose of this final book of the Bible is to reveal the events which must come to pass before all God's promises have been fulfilled. At the very beginning we are told clearly the authority that the Apostle John had been given to write this unique book, was by God Himself. There is also a clear progression listing each responsible for the importance and accuracy of this exceptional book. These are now listed: The Lord God our Father in Heaven, 1:1-4, His Son, the Lord Jesus Christ, 1:1-2, 5-8, 10-20, the Holy Spirit, 1:10, the Apostle John, 1;1, the seven Churches, 1:20, and finally onto all those who read or hear and keep the words of this book, there is a special blessing, 1:3.   Its message is to all Christians everywhere throughout all the ages.

2. The introduction to the Message sent to the Seven Churches. 1:4-20.

(a) The essential importance of worshipping the Three Persons of the Trinity, 1:4-6.

This book starts with The Lord Jesus in Glory. The result of this is that many spiritual gifts are showered upon those who are worthy to receive the blessings that are given to those who have honoured their Saviour. Our Saviour and Lord was the "Firstfruits from among the dead", 1 Cor 15:20 &23. There is a continual emphasis upon the importance of The Trinity: the Everlasting God, the Seven Spirits and Jesus Christ.

Most of the books within the New Testament commence with the author's name or title and the Book of Revelation is the same. This book has the highest authorship possible as it is from "Him who is and who was and who is to come, and from the seven Spirits who are before His throne, and from Jesus Christ, the faithful witness, the firstborn from the dead". He is also the one who has the "total control over all the kings of the earth", He is also the "One who loved us and washed us from our sins in His own blood", 1:5. Not only has He cleansed us from our sin He "has made us kings and priests to His God and Father, to Him be glory and dominion forever and ever, Amen, 1:6."

Throughout this Book there is a constant emphasis upon the importance of the Holy Spirit. In the list of the seven churches each one has the same special challenge "He that has an ear let him hear what the Spirit says the churches", 2:7, 2:11, 2:17, 2:29, 3:6, 3:13 & 3:22. There are also six references showing clearly that the Holy Spirit guides and controls the work of God's servants. Four of these are concerned with John, 1:10, 4:2, 17:3, and 21:10, and the remaining are concerned with the Saints who are the Bride of Christ, 14:13 & 22:17. The Book of the Revelation also introduces another special title concerning the Holy Spirit and this is that of "the Seven Spirits" which is used instead of the usual "Holy Spirit". This title occurs four times in Revelation but not in any other part of scripture. In the first reference, 1:4-5, the "Seven Spirits" are given equality with the Lord Jesus Christ. In the next reference, 3:1, the "Seven Spirits" have a special responsibility for the dead church of Sardis. Then at 4:5, the "Seven Spirits of God" are the "Seven lamps burning before the Throne". Finally, there are the "Seven Spirits of God sent out into all the earth", 5:6. We are also told that the Seven Spirits of God are equated with the seven Eyes of the Lamb".

The Roman background at the time of the writing of the book of the Revelation was that of the Emperor Domitian (AD 81-96) who attempted to execute everyone who was known to be a Christian. It was under this severe background that those who were faithful to their Lord and Saviour were promised "Grace and Peace". This is not the peace that the world gives which is merely a temporary action which soon collapses. As our Lord told His disciples, "My peace I give you, not as the world so I give unto you. Let not your heart be troubled, neither let it be afraid", John 14:27.

(b) The Second Coming, 1:7-8.

As we shall see later in detail, 19:11-16, this refers to the final return to this earth of our Lord in power. At His ascension it is recorded only a few faithful followers witnessed this amazing event. It is recorded that "He was taken up and a cloud received Him out of their sight", Acts 1:9. At His return "He is coming with clouds and every eye shall see Him, even those who pierced Him", 1:7. Clear facts of this coming event was promised in detail to God's people, many years before He became a Man in order to die for our sins. Daniel records "Behold, One like the Son of Man, Coming with the clouds of heaven! Then to Him was given dominion and glory and a kingdom, which shall not pass away", Dan 7:13-14. Also given to Zechariah was the promise, "I will pour on the house of David and on the inhabitants of Jerusalem the Spirit of grace and supplication; then they will look on Me whom they pierced. Yes, they mourn for Him as one mourns for his only son", Zech 12:10.   As we shall see later in our studies, there is a clear distinction between the "Rapture" and the "Second Coming of our Lord".

3.   John's first vision, 1:9-16.

The Apostle John had been banished to the island of Patmos by the Emperor Domitian who caused so much suffering amongst the Christians and the Jews. It is still known today by the same name. There is no doubt he suffered severe persecution together with many others who were faithful in their love of Jesus their Lord, 1:9.

He stated, "I was in the Spirit on the Lord's Day", 1:10. It was a great way of introducing that all he wrote and all that he did was controlled by His Lord. This special day was unique and it was the start of the most amazing revelation that had ever been given to mankind by the One Who referred to Himself as "The Alpha and Omega, the First and the Last", 1:10-11. The Lord revealed to John that he had a very special responsibility to proclaim a unique message to each of the seven churches that were listed in chapters two and three of the commencement of the great prophesies.

(a) The seven golden lamp-stands, 1:12. An important aspect of the Tabernacle was the seven pure gold lamps, Ex 37:17-24. The vision that is given by Zechariah also has a number of parallels with the Book of Revelation, this includes a special golden lamp-stand which has seven lamps in the Temple, Zech 4:1-2. This is also prophetically involved with the two special witnesses, 11:3-6 & Zech 4:11-14.

(b) The vision "of One like the Son of Man". This special vision was revealed to John in, 1:13-18. He was now being prepared for the great task of writing down at God's command, in this unique book. Such a tremendous event was absolutely over whelming, and John records, "When I saw Him, I fell at His feet as dead", 1:17. Both Isaiah and Ezekiel had a similar vision with an identical result to that of John on the Isle of Patmos, Is 6:1-9 & Ezek 1:25-28. After the result of such an amazing vision our Lord gives John this essential encouragement, "Do not be afraid, I am the First and the Last". The vision continues as our Lord reminds John he is now face to face with the Almighty Lord and Saviour.

John is now given the authority and responsibility to make a true and accurate copy of all that will be revealed in this special book, 1:19-20. This passage then closes with an introduction to the seven churches.

The Church Era. Chapters 2 & 3. Fivefold message:

(a) To the church as named.
(b) Historical Background.
(c) To all individual churches throughout the ages.

(d) To all individual Christians including ourselves, and

(e) Prophesy for the history of the development of the Church until the Rapture.

1. EPHESUS. 2:1-7

(a) "He who holds the seven stars in His right hand, and who walks in the midst of the seven golden lamp-stands."

(b) Ephesus: Like many other historical areas it is now in total ruins. This is the combined result of natural erosion, many severe wars and also the effect of earthquakes. Tradition states that John was the Bishop of Ephesus and that Ephesus was the "Mother Church" of that province. It was also the site of the Temple of Diana which also resulted in considerable immorality and worship of the Occult. Despite the severe background of the Church it was well taught as is seen by a study of the Epistles of the "Ephesians" and "1 & 2 Timothy".

(c) They showed perseverance and patience. They also hated the false teaching especially the deeds of the Nicolaitanes. God hates false teaching and we must also hate the things that God hates. Despite this they still had a serious fault, in that they had lost their first love and had drifted away from their closeness with their Lord and Saviour. They were given a severe warning that unless they repented, their "candlestick" (referring to their witness) would be removed. They had relied on their past experiences and as a result they lost their love for Christ, their love for each other and their love for the lost.

(d) To the one who overcomes I will give to eat of the "Tree of Life". This refers to the Tree of Life in the Garden of Eden which led to sin and man being cast out of Paradise, Gen 3:1-24. The Tree of Life will be restored, see 22:2 & 14. See also the reference to the "Tree of Life", 2:7. The "Cross" of Calvary is also referred to as a "Tree". This is the same word in the Greek. See also Acts 10:39, Gal 3:13 & 1 Pet 2:24.

(e) AD 33-100. They were doctrinally correct as well as being zealous but they were wayward. However they hated the deeds of the Nicolaitanes, which God also hated.

2. SMYRNA. 2:8-11.

(a) "The First and the Last, who was dead and came to life".

(b) Smyrna is now known as Izmir, and continues to be a thriving city. It has been an important city with a history dating back approximately 3000 years. There was much idolatry as is seen by the Temples of Zeus and of Cybele, known as the Mother of the gods. One very severe problem was that of the worship of the Emperor who claimed to be God himself and demanded worship from all.

(c) They were still faithful under tribulation and poverty. Although they were poor as far this world's goods were concerned, they were rich in the blessings showered upon them by God. There is no criticism of their way of life. They are warned that the day of severe persecution is near but they are urged to be faithful until death.

(d) The one who overcomes shall not be hurt by the second death. This promise is reiterated later in chapter 20:6.

(e) AD 100-312. This was a time of severe martyrdom under Rome.

3. PERGAMOS. 2:12-17.

(a) "He who has the sharp two-edged sword".

(b) Pergamos was known as "Satan's Throne", which was a very severe condemnation. Parallel with this, it was also the centre of the Roman Government which was based upon the worship of the Roman Emperor. There was a Temple to Octavius Caesar and every year all must offer incense to the Emperor and declare him to be God. All were controlled by political power and pagan worship, with an emphasis on academic and philosophical studies. This is now the town of Bergama.

(c) There are those who were truly faithful such as Antipas who was a martyr. There were others who were given a strong condemnation as their city was the one in which Satan dwelt. Parallel with this, there were also those who were far from being faithful which led to the sacrificing to idols and also to sexual immorality. We are told that "Balaam loved the wages of unrighteousness", 2 Pet 2:15, Jude 11 & Acts 15:28-29. In addition to this there were those "who held to the doctrine of the Nicolaitans, where Satan's Throne is". As well as this, they had pressure from outside by false Jews. Satan attacked by

minted. It was later ruled by Croesus who was known for his extreme wealth. It was captured by the Persians around BC 400 and destroyed by an earthquake in AD 17. It was rebuilt by Tiberius Caesar in AD 17 and a Temple to Cybele became one of their main forms of false worship. It was finally destroyed in AD 1402 and today there are only extensive ruins remaining of this great city.

(c) Sardis had no good spiritual overall aspect, just a minority of those who were truly faithful. It was a sleeping church which claimed to be alive but God said that they were spiritually dead. As a result of this, He called them to repent of their way of life.

(d) He who overcomes shall be clothed in white garments and I will not blot out his name from the Book of Life, but I will confess his name before My Father and before His angels.

(e) AD 1517-1750. The era of Reformation. They were reformed but not revived because they did not shake off elaborate rituals and human traditions.

6. PHILADELPHIA. 3:7-13.

(a) "He who is holy, He who is true".

(b) In Philadelphia there was still a good Christian witness until recently, but at present there appears to be considerable pressure by Muslim leaders and as a result there is increasing persecution today amongst many true Christians. This is a real "sign of the latter days" as this situation is increasing rapidly worldwide as we approach the final church in Laodicea.

The location of Philadelphia is now named the town of Ala-Shehir. It was destroyed by the same earthquake that destroyed Sardis in AD 17, but it was rebuilt by Tiberius Caesar. It was a wine growing district and this led to an emphasis upon the worship of Bacchus, the "god of wine".

(c) They kept the Lord's commandments to persevere, and they were faithful and received no criticism. They also resisted the "Synagogue of Satan" 3:9, see also 2:9. As this is the last but one of the build-up of the Lord's special messages to the Churches, the Lord Jesus gives a special promise that "He is coming quickly", 3:11. He also gives them a promise to keep them from (not through) the coming trial upon the whole earth. Is there just a hint here that the true Church will be removed from this earth before the terrible time of the Tribulation? Later we will see that there will be a clear emphasis upon this great truth.

(d) To he who overcomes I will make him a pillar in the temple of My God. I will write on him the name of My God and the name of the city of My God.

(e) AD 1750-1925. Revivals and Missionary era, e.g. China Inland Mission, Salvation Army, Wesley, Whitefield, Finney, Spurgeon, Moody, and many others. A steady decline from 1918 onwards affected the majority of true

Christians. A personal comment by the author is that I believe that God gave our country and a number of others a further opportunity to return to Him during and immediately after the Second World War.

7   LAODICEA. 3:14-22.

(a) "The Amen, the Faithful and True Witness, the Beginning of the creation of God".

(b) Laodicea was a rich city which specialised in banking, textiles and eye ointment. This was near to or connected with Colossae, Col 4:13-16. Today it is in total ruins.

(c) The situation described here is identical to that which we see amongst the many professing Christians today. This is the final message leading us into the special teaching of the very last days. The situation today teaches us that many are concerned with money and all that money can buy. God warns them and us that although we consider ourselves to be wealthy, "we are wretched, miserable, poor, blind and naked". This situation is because we have relied on material blessings. Despite our wealth, in God's sight "we are wretched, miserable and poor". Laodicea was famous for the manufacture of a special eye salve but God warns that despite this, they were "blind". God also warns them that they were also "naked" although they were one of the most important manufacturers of textiles. They are a lukewarm church who were "Rich (materially) but poor (spiritually)". God warns us that we are also in danger of allowing worldly situations to become our aim in life.

(d) "Behold I stand and knock", 3:20. This is one of the best known passages in all Scripture and it has been a blessing to many who have been converted by reading this verse. If we now look again at this wonderful passage of scripture, it may also be applied to the second coming where those who are ready and waiting for the coming of the Lord are gathered together into His Presence. This is especially so because this is the final passage in Revelation which leads directly into the division between those who are ready and waiting for their Lord's return and those who are not ready.

(e) AD 1926 and onwards to the rapture and to God's great plan for the future. This now refers to the present situation but we have no knowledge whatever of how long it will be before our Lord returns for us. "To him who overcomes I will grant to sit with Me on My Throne, as I also overcame and sat down with My Father on His throne". This is a direct statement stating that those who are ready are granted an entry into the Presence of the Lord God Himself.

(f) The final situation around us now is also the time of Biblical Criticism; Philosophical Rationalism; Self-sufficiency; the increasing rise of false religion parallel with a decreasing acceptance of true Biblical Christianity. Finally there is compromise and worldliness all leading us to the time of the Great Tribulation.

C. THE RAPTURE AND THE EFFECT UPON HEAVEN AND EARTH.

From 4:1 through to 20:6 there are two vitally important events which are the Rapture and the Return of the Lord Jesus to this earth to set up His Kingdom. As we shall see, these two amazing events together with a number of other essential developments are clearly defined in this section of God's Word. It also states quite clearly whether each of these events are in Heaven (the abode of Almighty God) or whether they are on this earth. There are also some locations clearly stated to be in Hell, the abode of evil demons and Satan himself. In order to locate the situation of each section, a special heading will be given in the centre of the page using one of the following: **HEAVEN, EARTH** or **HELL.**

LOCATED IN HEAVEN.

1. The Throne of Almighty God. 4:1–11.

John is now in Heaven (the abode of God) not on earth, 4:1. He is invited to "Come up here" and God promises him that, "I will show you things which must take place after this". Previously to this present time many of the prophecies of the "last days" were not understood. Even Daniel was not able to understand the full implications of the prophecies that God had given to him as these were "sealed till the last days", Dan 12:8-10. But now God's revelations will become clearer as events unfold. This is God's last word to us therefore He will include everything that we need to know concerning the future. From this verse forward this prophecy is involved only with the future. Because of this there is now no mention of the Church on this earth until chapter 19:11-21. However there are a few special messengers that are sent to this earth to present God's final call to repentance.

This state's quite clearly that a throne is set up in Heaven and this indicates that there is supreme authority over all, 4:2. Isaiah 6:1-4, Jeremiah 3:17 and Ezekiel 1:4-28 each had a similar revelation.

There are clear comparisons with this throne (4:3) and also the one detailed in Ezekiel 1:28. Both referred to a rainbow over the throne. Ezekiel states that this was the appearance of the likeness of the Glory of the Lord. The importance of the rainbow reminds us of God's promise to Noah, Gen 9:12-17.

"Twenty-four elders were clothed in white robes, wearing crowns of gold and sitting around the throne", 4:4. The term "elder" is of special significance for the Church, see 1 Tim 5:17 & Titus 1:5. As we will see under 5:9, at this stage the Church has already been raptured and is now in Heaven in the presence of God.

"There is thunder and lightning proceeding from the throne", 4:5. This concept of God's tremendous authority is repeated again under 8:5, 11:19 & 16:18. In addition there are the "Seven lamps of fire… burning before the throne, which are the seven Spirits of God". The seven golden candlesticks were originally on earth (1:13) but are now in Heaven (4:5). This is another confirmation that the Church has been raptured and is now in Heaven, see 5:9. When God gave the Ten Commandments to Moses on Mt Sinai similar circumstances were present. "There were thundering and lightings" and "Mount Sinai was completely enveloped in smoke, because the Lord descended upon it in fire", see Exodus 19:16-18.

"A sea of glass, like crystal", see 4:6-9. This is descriptive of a vast number of people. This is also setting the pattern for the vast number of those who were now in the presence of their Lord, see also 5:11-13. The "sea of glass" indicates a perfectly calm sea referring to those who are at peace with God, see also 15:2.

This now introduces four beasts each with six wings. These creatures are special and although other similar creatures have been created, there are often important similarities between them in their responsibility to worship Almighty God. In this group there are a total of four special living creatures. The first was like a lion, the second was like a calf, the third had a face like a man and the forth was like a flying eagle. In addition they each had six wings and they were full of eyes around and within (4:6-10). They never slept at any time but announced "Holy, holy, holy, Lord God Almighty, Who was and is to come!"

There are two similar events recorded in the Old Testament and the first of these is in Isaiah 6:2. The special creatures described here are stated to be seraphim, which is a term that is used only in Isaiah chapter 6 and not found anywhere else in the whole of scripture. Their responsibility was to reveal the holiness of God and this led to Isaiah realising that he was a sinner before God. The other special event is in Ezekiel 1:5-12 and 10:18-22 which refers to four Living Creatures. There are both important similarities as well as differences. The main difference was that each Living Creature had four faces. The similarities (compared with Revelation) were that four Living Creatures had the face of a man, the face of a lion, the face of an ox and the face of an eagle, Three of the them were identical apart from the "Ox" in Ezekiel which was similar to the "Calf" of Revelation.

Immediately following this, the twenty-four elders "give glory and honour and thanks to Him Who sits on the throne and Who lives forever and ever", 4:10-11. He is also the One who created all. The importance of the "Twenty-four Elders" is emphasised by the number of times they are mentioned. See 4:4, 4:10, 5:8, 5:14, 11:16 & 19:4. In addition, the same "Elders" are mentioned in 7:11 & 14:3 but we are not told that there are twenty-four. Usually, but not always, they were linked with the four Living Creatures. These are obviously twenty-four special people and one possible interpretation is that they are representatives of the twelve tribes of Israel and the twelve apostles. A hint of this is found in 21:12 & 14 see note at that reference.

2. The Adoration of the Lamb. 5:1–14.

The sealed scroll, 5:1-4. It was normal procedure to apply a number of seals to prevent unauthorised tampering with a scroll. This scroll was protected by seven seals indicating that this contained vital information which could be read only by someone who was able to break all the seals. This was such an important scroll that there appeared to be no one able to open the scroll nor even permitted to merely look at it.

Only One, the Lord Jesus Christ was worthy to open the seals, 5:5-8. He is given two vital Titles, "The Lion of the Tribe of Judah" and "The Root of David". The term "Root of David" occurs only here and in chapter 22:16. The meaning of "Root" is that of "stock, family or descendant". This reminds one of the humanity of our Lord which was absolutely essential for His Crucifixion at Calvary. The essential importance of this is also seen by the phrase, "He stood as a Lamb that had been slain", 5:6.

We are now given the answer to a problem that has been discussed many times yet there are many Christians who do not accept what is stated quiet clearly in the next few verses as well as in several other passages of Scripture, 5:9-10. We read: "You are worthy to take the scrolls and to open its seals; for you were slain, and have redeemed us to God by your blood out of every tribe and tongue and people and nation. And have made us kings and priests to our God: and we shall reign on the earth". There is no doubt whatever that the many millions of people who are worshipping their Redeemer are in His very Presence which is in Heaven, the abode of Almighty God, see 4:1-8. There is one essential phrase which needs to be understood and this is "We shall reign on the earth", 5:10. This does not state that they will reign at that particular time, the use of the word "shall" indicates an event that may still be in the future at that time. This is later revealed in detail in 20:4-6.

This is the final summary of the first stage of the greatness of the Lord Jesus Christ as the millions cry out, "Worthy is the Lamb who was slain to receive power, and riches, and wisdom, and strength, and honour, and glory and blessing!" 5:11-14. The final climax leads to the worship by the entire angelic host as well as those who have been redeemed.

D. THE TRIBULATION PERIOD. THE LAMB IS IN HEAVEN BUT THE RESULT OF OPENING THE SEALS CONCERN THE EVENTS UPON EARTH.

1. The First to the Sixth Seals are now listed. 6:1-17

In order to understand the importance of the seven seals, see note above at 5:1-8.

Ch 6:1-17 & 8:1-5. The first four seals are also known as the "Four Horses of the Apocalypse". The seventh seal leads straight into the "seven trumpets", and details are given at 8:1-5.

(a) The first seal, 6:1-2. The opening of the first seal reveals a rider upon a white horse who sets out to be the Conqueror of the world. In chapter 19:11-21 there is a reference to a similar Horse where the Rider is the "Faithful and True" and the context of this states that this is the Lord Jesus returning in power. We must be absolutely clear that there is a vital difference between these two unique situations.

The context of the horse and rider of the first seal shows clearly that he is either the Antichrist or his predecessor. In the epistles of John we have the only references to the actual name of the Antichrist. John also warned that "You have heard that the Antichrist is coming, even now many Antichrists have come, by which we know that it is the last hour", 1 John 2:18-19. It may be that these four horsemen are all different aspects of the final Antichrist. Whoever this rider may be, he is setting the pattern from whom the final Antichrist will develop. As we shall see later, the real Antichrist will be the one who appears to be able to duplicate the power and authority of our Lord for a short time.

(b) The second seal, 6:3-4. A fiery red horse is responsible for war or rather anarchy. There was obviously peace upon earth at the start of this second seal, but this is replaced by tribulation and then war. The fact that the horse was "red" may indicate that this refers to Russia with their Arab allies. See also "the final satanic rebellion" which occurs after the return of Christ to this earth, see 20:7-10. It is likely that Israel will be attacked at this time.

(c) The third seal, 6:5-6. A black horse brings famine and injustice which is often the result of war or anarchy. This indicates severe shortages of basic foods at inflated prices because one quart of wheat will cost an entire day's wages. But there will be plenty of luxuries such as oil and wine for those who can afford them. Today there is an Increasing worldwide spread of famine throughout the world and parallel with this there is a minority that are rapidly increasing their wealth. This may be caused by a whole range of situations such as war; threats of war; unemployment; increasing costs of food and transport; reduction of wages; together with natural disasters.

(d) The fourth seal, 6:7-8. A pale horse brings death which is the final result of the three previous horsemen. A quarter of the entire population is killed by war, famine, disease and wild animals. The final rider of the forth horse has the name of "Death and Hades" which indicates only unbelievers will perish at this stage.

(e) The fifth seal, 6:9-11. This is concerned with those who were still living upon the earth and who remained faithful during the Tribulation period and as a result suffered severely. These would be those who were not ready when the Lord came for His own but who have now repented of their sinful ways and were now seeking to serve the true God. A similar situation is also revealed immediately after the sixth seal 7:1-17 and during the opening of the seventh seal 8:2-6. This would be a very difficult time for all of those seeking to obey God because the Church is no longer on earth as it is now in Heaven, as we have already noted under 4:1-5:14. As the Holy Spirit has a special relationship with the true Church, it would appear highly likely that the Holy Spirit would be withdrawn when the Church was raptured. There would still be those who eventually realised their error and as a result refused to have the mark of the Antichrist. See also 7:1-3

(f) The sixth seal, 6:12-17. From this stage there is an increasing level of the judgement which God pours out upon the earth. This is a very severe earthquake resulting in widespread damage yet there is still more to come. Parallel with the earthquake there was also an out-pouring of the judgement of God upon the sun which became black, the moon became like blood, the stars fell to the earth, and the sky was radically changed. In their terror, those who remained alive fled to the mountains and the islands, in the vague hope that they may be offered some protection. We see later in 8:5, 11:13 and 16:18 that there are similar judgements to follow that are even far worse. There have been many interpretations and debates concerning what exactly the form of this judgement will take. All we can understand is that these are special judgements which are poured out upon a rebellious world by an all-powerful, Holy God.

Our Lord gave us a severe warning that one of the marks of the last days would be "famines, pestilences and earthquakes", Mt 24:7; Mk 13:8 and Lk 21:11 and we have seen that this situation is increasing both in frequency and in power. Our passage in Revelation 6:12-17 demonstrates that these are terrible warnings to a world that has defied the Lord God. We see here a special basis of God's severe judgement as those on earth cry to the mountains and rocks, "Fall on us and hide us from the face of Him who sits on the throne and from the wrath of the Lamb". Men's reactions were not towards repentance but total fear, hiding in the rocks and praying to them instead of to God Himself. This reminds us that the Lamb of God is no longer on earth but in His rightful place in Heaven where He is worshipped by the heavenly Host. Why is this severe judgement poured upon those who are now living upon the earth? He came as the "Lamb of God who takes away the sin of the world" (John 1:29). As we seek out the special message that God gives us in this wonderful book, we see that the "Day of Grace" is no longer available to those who have rejected the Lord Jesus. We do however see that there are those from the nation of Israel who, in those last days will turn to God in true repentance.

E. THE SEALING OF CONVERTED JEWS ON EARTH WHO ARE THEN TAKEN UP TO HEAVEN.

2. The 144,000 are saved from Israel for a special responsibility. 7:1-8.

The book of Revelation is mainly concerned with judgement rather than admonition, but even then in the early part of the tribulation there are still those severe warnings which come from a Holy God. Parallel with this we still see God calling His people to atonement. This however will not be an easy way out for those who have ignored the call of repentance. It will have to be followed by a blameless life and one that will almost certainly end in martyrdom. In chapter 7 there are the first two of these special responsibilities of being chosen to do some special work for God.

This section commences with the choosing of 144,000 special servants for conveying God's distinct message of repentance to those in the earth. All judgement is withheld until the servants of God are sealed. These are the Tribulation Saints chosen by God to be the Jewish evangelists to those living during the tribulation, 7:2-3. In order to seal these servants, the coming destruction of earth, sea and trees is postponed for a short time. The meaning of the "Sealing" of these saints refers to an exceptional protection given by God Himself.

A unique distinguishing mark is placed upon the forehead of all of God's true Servants. Later the Antichrist demands that all of his followers also have an identification mark on their foreheads see 13:16-18. Also nothing is permitted to damage the whole realm of nature until the servants of God are ready. There is also a special reference to the restraint of the weather 7:3. These 144,000 are protected till the end of the completion of their special task, see 14:1-5. Are these the "Brothers" of Matt 25:31-46? There will be a spiritual vacuum left by the Rapture despite lies told by Antichrist, as there will be those who realise the terrible choice that they have made.

The sealing of the faithful 144,000 who are chosen from Jewish people during the Tribulation for their faithfulness despite the severe presure to backslide. The origin of the twelve tribes was based upon the twelve sons of Jacob but the tribe of Joseph was given a double portion and divided into Ephraim and Manasseh. Also the Tribe of Levi was given the oversight of the Tabernacle and the Offerings, as they were considered to be a holy tribe and were not now included with the remainder of the tribes. The list here is divided into twelve groups, but there is no mention of the tribe of Dan and Ephraim in this list. It has been suggested that this maybe is because they were the first tribes to become the centres of idolatry in Israel. See Judges 18:30-31 & 1 Kings 12:28-33. In this list, the tribes of Dan and Ephraim are replaced by that of Joseph and Levi. The meaning of the number 12,000 for each tribe does not necessarily have a unique significance. See 14:1 for "144,000 in Presence of the Lamb".

3. Triumphant multitude of the redeemed in Heaven. 7:9-17.

This is a different group from those listed of the chosen from the 144,000 Jewish people. These are chosen from all the nations and ethnic groups but we are not given the number of this vast multitude, 7:9. These have come through the "Great Tribulation", 7:14. This is not merely "any tribulation" which is a part of what all of God's people must expect from time to time, see also John 16:33, Acts 14:22. We have already seen that the rapture has taken place. See "C. The Rapture and the Effect upon Heaven and Earth", 4:1-5:15. This therefore is now the start of the Great Tribulation, see Matt 24:21, Mk 13:24 & Jer 30:7, and the situation is far worse than anything that has taken place previously. But even then, as we will see, the situation will rapidly deteriorate. Our loving God is now offering an opportunity to those who have previously turned their back on Him to be cleansed from their sin in the Blood of the Lamb. This is only for those who are willing to repent of their sin and come to Him in true repentance knowing that they will face a martyr's death, see 7:13-17.

F. THE LAMB IS IN HEAVEN AND BUT THE RESULT OF OPENING OF THE SEALS CONCERNS THE EVENTS UPON EARTH.

4. The Introduction to the Seven Trumpets. 8:1-4.

The seventh seal leads to the seven trumpets. For a comparison between the trumpets and the bowls of God's wrath see note on chapter 16.

Seal 7. There is silence in Heaven for about half an hour. This is the lull before the storm which will develop into the pouring out of the wrath of God. Contrast the silence here with the loud praises of 7:9-14. The offering of the incense is the acceptance by the Lord God of the prayers of His saints.

5. The Seven Trumpets. 8:5-11:19.

The silence is broken as another angel is given the power to cast "noises, thundering, lightening and an earthquake upon the earth". The seven angels are now ready to commence the seven trumpet judgements, 8:5-6. There appears to be two distinct divisions and the first division is the first, second, third and fourth trumpets. The second division is the fifth, sixth and seventh trumpets.

(a) The first trumpet sounded and "hail and fire mixed with blood is cast upon the earth and a third of all the trees together with all the grass is destroyed". 8:7. This could obviously be the result of a very severe earthquake or volcano. On the other hand it could also be the result of a nuclear explosion or even something entirely new. The destruction of all trees and grass would be disastrous as this would destroy all corn, wheat, oats, rice, etc. These are basic food for both humans and animals. The concept that this severe judgement results in total annihilation of one third of all grass, crops and trees would be utterly devastating. Other serious effects would also be the problems of pollution. A similar pattern repeats itself on each of the remaining second, third and fourth trumpet judgements.

(b) The second trumpet judgement reveals "something like a great mountain burning with fire which was thrown into the sea and a third of the sea became blood. A third of all creatures in the sea died and a third of all ships were destroyed". 8:8-9. This could be a severe tropical storm, a tsunami, a nuclear bomb (a powerful Inter Continental Ballistic Missile may have looked like this to John), or it could obviously be something quite unknown to us now. This would result in a third of the sea becoming polluted as if by blood. In addition, a third of the living creatures inhabiting the sea died. In many countries fish is the main source of food, so this would result in widespread starvation. Finally one third of all ships were also destroyed. Not only would this cause the considerable death of many seamen and travellers, it would also cause the considerable loss of valuable cargo. Many countries rely on their navy for protection. Once more God does not permit total destruction at this stage. Reducing the judgement to only one third once more shows God's love and mercy even to those who have rejected Him. See Ez 38:22-23 where a similar judgement is poured upon Gog and Magog.

(c) The third trumpet warns of a "great star falling from heaven and causing severe pollution upon one third of the rivers and the fresh springs of water", 8:10-11. Again this is a harsh judgement effecting one third of all drinking water causing many to die as a result of drinking the only water available which was severely polluted. The number of those who were poisoned by this water was not restricted to a third as it states clearly that many died because they drank this polluted water. In ancient languages such as Hebrew the title of "star" may also apply to a whole range of heavenly bodies such as a "comet" or "asteroid". This then could be an asteroid, or a comet, or even something quite new and unknown by us today. Any of these could easily produce this type of situation that is given to us in our reading. Nevertheless we must never be dogmatic over any suggestions which may have other acceptable proposals.

(d) The fourth trumpet is concerned with the partial destruction of the sun, the moon and the stars, and is once more based upon the partial destruction of one third, 8:12-13. There are several similarities between the fourth trumpet and the sixth seal (see 6:12-17), although it would appear that as we progress through these prophecies that they often have similar teachings which becomes increasingly more severe. Such a relentless situation may result from a variety of causes such as a break up of a comet or other similar natural phenomena. It could also be the result of nuclear fallout, a severe dust storm, or a volcanic disturbance. It may be a special miracle of which we have no knowledge at this stage. Darkness in Scripture is often associated with the judgment of a Holy God, see Ex 10:21-29, Is 13:9-10, Ezek 30:18, Joel 3:14-16, Mt 24:29 & Mt 27:45.

(e) A comparison of the first four trumpets and the three later trumpets. The first four trumpets were directed towards ecology, but the last three are directed towards mankind. The last three trumpets present a severe warning that there is much worse to come, 8:13. John states that he heard an angel crying out, "Woe, woe, woe to the inhabitants because of the remaining blasts of the trumpet". This would indicate that judgement is steadily increasing, causing terrible results far worse than anything known previously.

(f) The fifth trumpet and the first woe, 9:1-12. John sees a star fall from Heaven onto the earth. See comment on meaning of "star" under third trumpet (c) above. The Angel was given the responsibility of opening the bottomless pit sometimes referred to in Scripture as the Abyss. Up to this situation everything (apart from a brief reference in 5:3) has been either in Heaven or on this Earth, but from this point in our studies the location is introduced which is the bottomless pit, 9:1 & 2. The general meaning of this word means "the abode of demons" but it is not the place of final judgement and should not therefore be confused with the "Lake of Fire". A new stage in our studies now opens up an entirely different range of severe judgements, as God permits Satan and his slaves to have the ability to achieve evil deeds. We must realise that the Lord God remains in supreme control of all events and of all living creatures whether in Heaven, in earth or even in the bottomless pit. We are concerned here with the result of the bottomless pit being opened in order to release the plague of special locusts upon those who have continued to defy the commandments of the Almighty God. For other important references to the bottomless pit and the terrible inhabitants which we will review later, see 11:7, 17:8 & 20:1 & 3.

The plague of the "killer" locusts could refer to the tormenting demons led by Apollyon, the Destroyer. He is probably not Satan himself but a fallen angel who is also very powerful. The fifth angel was given the key to the bottomless pit so that he could release these special "locusts". It is clear by the description of these "locusts" in verses 3 to 11, that these are no ordinary insects but something quite unique. Although they are called "locusts" they are not permitted to harm the grass, nor any tree, neither may they damage any vegetation, but they are ordered to pour severe torment upon those who have defied Almighty God. Previously to this, they existed only in the bottomless pit being imprisoned by the authority of the Lord God. To see further details of "fallen angels", see also 2 Peter 2:4-5 & Is 14:12-17. It is also doubtful if this refers to the same person as the "fallen star" of 9:1.

Various suggestions have been proposed concerning the details of these "locusts". A selection of these include demonic activity, chemical or germ warfare (such as helicopters with nerve gas spray), or even mutant locusts. It may be something quite new that God has reserved for those last terrible days. Parallel with this is the increasing activity and power of Satan which is also a mark of the last days. Why use the locust as a mark of those horrific final times? John simply wrote down something which he saw that was something quite new, yet there are some aspects which he could understand. The locust is probably the most destructive of all creation. The results of trumpets 5 to 7 now become far more destructive than those of numbers 1 to 4. Those having the "Seal of God" (compare also chapter 7) are protected indicating that a "Remnant" is still on earth. It is the result of the plague of locusts that is so important rather than speculation upon what or who they are.

(g) The sixth trumpet and the second woe. 9:13-21. The sixth angel is commanded to "Release the four angels who are bound at the great river Euphrates". These four angels "had already been prepared for an hour, a day, a month and a year, and they were now released to kill all mankind". In this Second Woe there is a special emphasis concerning the River Euphrates. The Euphrates has great importance in both Scripture and in the study of secular history because it is the natural barrier between the East and the West. At 1780 miles it is the longest and the most important river in Western

Asia. It was one of the four rivers that watered Eden (Gen 2:14) and had therefore a special part within the creation of this world. Because of the fact that sin then entered the Garden of Eden this beautiful river also became tainted with sin but it still has an important influence in God's plan for the future. It was also a part of the special land that God promised to Abraham, Gen 15:18, Deut 1:7 & 11:24. This was confirmed again when the Children of Israel entered the Promised Land under the leadership of Joshua, Josh 1:4. It was also the main river flowing through the city of Babylon from where God permitted Nebuchadnezzar to destroy Jerusalem and make slaves of the God's own people because of their sin, Jeremiah 46:10 & 51:63-64.

As the terrible situation at the time of the second woe deteriorates, we refer back to the four special angels who have been bound in the Euphrates to be released and to kill a third of mankind 9:14-17. A special army of two hundred million horsemen is now released for this terrible task. These however are no ordinary horsemen but something quite terrible and vastly different from anything that has already been used by God. A brief review of 9:17-19 would reveal that these are quite unique and have no parallels with anything else. They have many similarities with the locusts of the first woe that were sent upon those defying God. The sin of those is listed in detail in 9:20-21, and this was that they worshipped demons and false idols, committed murder, theft, sexual immorality and sorceries. We see many parallels with this sinfulness and the increasing development of all that God hates in the situation around today, which we believe are the last days before the rapture of those who are ready to meet their Lord and Saviour. See 16:12 where the sixth bowl of God's Wrath also refers to the Euphrates as a barrier to and from the East.

6. There is now an interlude between the Sixth Trumpet and the Seventh Trumpet. 10:1–11:13

(a) The mighty angel and the little book, 10:1-7. The name "Mighty Angel" is used only rarely and refers to special angels in 10:1, 18:21 and also 5:2 where an similar term of "strong" is used. This obviously means that these angels have special responsibilities. The mighty angel opened the book but before he was permitted to state what was in the message it was sealed. Daniel had a similar situation when he was given the prophecy referring to the last days and then ordered to "Shut up the words and seal the book until the end of time", Dan 12:4. The angel now states that "There should be no more delay". The completion of the judgement of a Holy God is drawing to the final stages and He will now reveal much that was hidden earlier.

(b) John eats the scroll of God's Word, 10:8-11. Ezekiel was given a similar experience at the commencement of his ministry, Ezek 2:8-3:4. To eat the book refers to John absorbing it and making it a part of himself. It was initially enjoyable, teaching us that God's Word should be a joy to read. Parallel with this, for those who read or hear the Word of God and reject it, it will become condemnation. For those who proclaim the true Word of God it will be seen to be a message of joy, therefore it will sadden those who have rejected its message. Man's sin and rejection of God's Word will result in bitterness. Despite this, John is told to continue to "prophesy again to many peoples, nations, tongues and kings". We have that same responsibility, we must still present the unadulterated message that we see and understand in His Word.

(c) A brief understanding of the Hebrew dating systems is essential for an understanding of these passages, 11:1-2. The term "one week" may be understood to mean either "seven days" or "seven years". It is revealed in Daniel 9:27 that the Antichrist will "make a covenant (or peace treaty) for one week". This therefore must be either seven days or seven years. The only acceptable time must be seven years for the overall control by the Antichrist. During the first half of this period of time the Temple will be rebuilt in Jerusalem. The Temple here is a false temple set up at the beginning of the Tribulation. The Temple referred to in the New Testament was destroyed in AD 70, but John had this vision in AD 95 so another temple will need to be built. This would indicate that the Jews will be permitted by the Antichrist to build another Temple therefore an agreement between them would be necessary. It is generally considered that the Antichrist will appear to be a "Man of Peace" when he first sets up his worldwide control.

Then after half of that time he will break his covenant especially with the Jewish Nation and take over as the world wide dictator. Throughout the Book of Revelation we are concerned mainly with the world control of the Antichrist who is usually referred to in Revelation as the "Beast".

The next stage is that "the holy city will be trodden underfoot for forty-two months" which is three and a half years. In the Book of Revelation this period of time is vital as it is listed five times as follows.

11:2.   "Forty two months", (three and a half years).

11:3.   "1260 days", (three and a half years).

12:6.   "1260 days", (three and a half years).

12:14.   "For a time and times and half a time",
         (1 + 2 + 0.5 = three and a half years).

13:5.   "Forty two months", (three and a half years).
         As we have just seen, the verses listed above are
         concerned with a simple understanding of the
         basis of the Hebrew system of dating. A knowledge
         of Hebrew grammar is not essential.

(d) We now return to the importance of the teaching of the olive trees and the two lamp stands, 11:3-6. These obviously refers to the earlier prophesy of Zechariah 4:1-14. This states that there will be "two anointed ones who stand beside the Lord of the whole earth". They have the power to do many miracles. "They will have the authority to prevent rain falling upon the earth, to turn water to blood and to strike the earth with severe plagues." These two true servants of God have the special responsibility of presenting the very last opportunity to repent that is given to those on earth. When their testimony is completed, the beast ascends from the bottomless pit and kills them. "Their dead bodies will lie in the street of the great city which spiritually is called Sodom and Egypt where our Lord was crucified", 11:8. (See also the 5th trumpet at (f) 9:1-12 for the bottomless pit.) These three locations are linked spiritually: Jerusalem was the place that God had chosen for those who truly sought Him, Sodom was the place of open sin and Egypt was the country that oppressed God's people Where our Lord was crucified is obviously Jerusalem, and although this was God's special chosen city for His own people in many instances they rebelled against Him. After three and a half days these two special servants are restored back to life and then caught up to Heaven.

Who are these unnamed witnesses? We do not know for certain but many Bible scholars have suggested that they could be Elijah and Moses. Apart from Peter, James and John, only Moses and Elijah were privileged to be with our Lord on the Mount of Transfiguration, which makes them unique. Our Lord also referred to John the Baptist as "He is Elijah who is to come", Matt 11:14. We also have the firm promise in Mal 4:5-6; "Behold I will send Elijah the prophet before the coming of the great and dreadful day of the Lord". In addition to this, Elijah was given the authority to be instrumental in causing a severe drought in Israel, 1 Kings 17:1. Other factors to consider are that Elijah did not die but was taken up to Heaven by a whirlwind, 2 Kings 2:1 and the death of Moses was also of a special nature, Deut 34:1-12. Moses represents the Law and Elijah represents the prophets. Also both were given the authority to work miracles. Whoever they are is not of prime importance, it is vital that we understand that they are God's very last final warning to the world using human agents. The final climax of this is a "Great Earthquake" in Jerusalem.

7. **The sounding of the final trumpet together with the third and final woe.**

MAINLY IN HEAVEN BUT EARTH IS ALSO INVOLVED.

(a) The sounding of the final trumpet reveals the closeness of the final return of the Lord Jesus Christ with His saints to this earth in power and authority. The emphasis upon the third and final woe is a severe warning that this will result in great calamity to all who have ignored the warnings revealed in this book.

The seventh and final trumpet and the third woe will now be released. The passage reveals that there are now tremendous changes about to take place, 11:14-19. First of all there is the third and final woe.

(b) The cry from Heaven reveals one of the most

spectacular events that will ever to take place. "The kingdoms of this world have become the kingdoms of our Lord and of His Christ and he shall reign forever and ever," 11:15. We reach now the final preparation of the judgement which will fall upon all the nations that have defied Almighty God.

The scene is now set in the "Temple of God" in Heaven, 11:19. When Moses made the original furnishings for the Tabernacle, He was shown the pattern of these in Heaven, Heb 8:5. These are obviously of vital importance, and may even be the originals chosen by God for a special purpose.

This prepares for the terrible future events that will soon be poured out upon this earth. These will include lightning, extreme noise, thunders, a severe earthquake, and great hail.

G. THE SCENE SET FOR THE FINAL SITUATION BEFORE THE RETURN OF CHRIST TO THIS EARTH.

THE NATURE OF SATAN, THE ANTICHRIST AND THE FALSE PROPHET. CHAPTERS 12.1 – 15:8.

1. **The Final days of the Authority and Power of Satan, the Red Dragon. 12:1-6.**

(a) We now approach the rebellion which will lead to the final defeat of Satan and his two associates, the Antichrist and the false prophet. They will set up their own concept of a trinity which is their final futile attempt to overcome the Authority of the true Trinity of the Father, the Son and the Holy Spirit.

(b) "A great sign appeared in Heaven, the woman clothed with the sun and wearing on her head a garland of twelve stars," 12:1.

(c) We now have a special sign that appeared in heaven which was a great, fiery red dragon having seven heads and ten horns. It had the ability to draw a third of the stars in the heavens and cast them onto the earth. At this stage we are not told any details concerning who this dragon is, but in chapters 12 to 13 there are eleven references to his utterly evil nature. This can apply only to Satan himself.

(d) We are not told the actual identity of the Child but we are told that He is caught up to God and His throne, and that

He will rule all nations. This can only refer to one Person, the Lord Jesus Christ, 12:5. Parallel with this the woman is given a place "prepared by God" for one thousand two hundred and sixty days, 12:6. This is a total of three and a half years, the same as that stated for the time of several other vital events.

(e) Some have suggested that the garland of twelve stars upon her head is similar to that of the goddess Europa which has been placed in a prominent position upon the Parliament buildings of the European Union. The real truth is most likely to be that the E.U. is falsely claiming that this verse refers to them and will not be used for the purposes of a Holy God.

2.   Satan thrown out of Heaven. 12:7-12.

(a) In order to understand this important event we must know the true location of Heaven. This is referred to in the early section of this book under "A. Setting the basis for our study"; paragraph 10; and subsection (ii). Even today there are several different titles used for the location of Heaven. The meaning here cannot refer to the special Abode of Almighty God. A review of the passage 4:1 to 5:14 will show clearly that Heaven is the abode of God Himself and the aspect that sets it apart from all other locations is the emphasis upon holiness. Throughout the Bible the sky is also referred to as heaven and this is demonstrated by the following references 12:3 and 12:4. In addition to this, our Lord stated, "I saw Satan fall like lightening from Heaven"

(b) We are now introduced to a very important situation whatever the location of Satan's heaven may be. He and his angels were cast down to this earth, 12:8-9. This is the beginning of the end of the eventual destruction of Satan and all of his followers.

(c) There is rejoicing in Heaven because "the kingdom of our God, and the power of His Christ have come" and Satan "has been cast down to this earth", 12:10-11.

(d) "The devil has come down to you, having great wrath, because he knows that he only has a short time", 12:12. Thus begins the start of the most horrific period of events that this world has ever known. As we shall see later, these events will lead to the total destruction of this world.

3. **Satan, who is also called the Devil, and also the dragon, attempts to kill the woman who was chosen by God for a special purpose. 12:13-17.**

(a) We are not informed of the actual identity of this special woman but we do know she was chosen by God for a very special responsibility. At this stage we know that the rapture has already taken place (see 5:9-10), but we also know that we still await the return of Christ to this earth, so all we can say is that it would appear very likely that she was a very special servant of God. The time factor of two and a half years is again reiterated (12:14), confirming that of 12:6.

(b) We also know that Satan hated this special woman and attempted to kill her, but she was miraculously protected, 12:13-17.

(c) The Dragon now attempts to destroy all the few faithful offspring of the woman that are remaining on this earth, 12:12-17. We see in this situation that Satan and the Dragon are endeavouring to destroy all the works of Almighty God. The Dragon is so arrogant that he still attempts to kill all those who are faithful and keep the commandments of God. "Rejoice O Heavens and you who dwell in them. Woe to the inhabitants of the earth and the sea. For the Devil has come down to you, having great wrath, because he knows that his time is short".

4.   The Beast from the Sea. 13:1-10.

Throughout chapter 12 we have seen that this is concerned with Satan himself but in chapter 13 we are introduced to two other very powerful evil beings that are subservient to Satan. These three form an evil trinity whose aim is to overthrow the true Trinity of the Father, the Son and the Holy Spirit.

(a) In the passage the second beast of this false trinity is seen to have a number of similarities compared with Daniel 7:3-7. In Daniel there are four beasts which are a lion, a bear, a leopard and finally an unnamed violent evil beast that obviously refers to a coming all powerful enemy. As we have seen earlier there have only been four main world powers, and there will be no more until the events that we are now studying become a reality. See details of this in the Introduction at the commencement of this book.

(b) The similarity between this passage and the one in Daniel 7:3-7 is unmistakable. The beast from the sea was like a leopard, but had the feet of a bear and the mouth of a lion. He also had seven heads and ten horns. In addition he was given great authority and power by the Dragon (also known as Satan). This second beast is the Antichrist although this title is not given throughout Revelation. One of his heads was mortally wounded, which would indicate that he was hated by some, but his deadly wound was healed. This led to amazement and to the majority of the entire population now worshipping the dragon and the beast. The beast was given the authority to remain in power for forty-two months which is three and a half years. This is the time that God permits the trinity of these three evil characters to have an apparent control over the whole earth, before He steps in to judge all those who have disobeyed and defied Him. This time is very important as it has already been stated in verses 11:2, 11:3, 12:6 and 12:14.

(c) The beast from the sea is now granted the ability to make war and kill all those saints who are still remaining upon this earth, 13:7-10. There is now a terrible situation remaining throughout the whole world because there are no saints remaining on the earth. This is such an important passage that the same phrase is used here that is used for each of the special messages that were sent to the seven churches in chapters two and three. "If anyone has an ear, let him hear". We see now that Satan and the Dragon are endeavouring to destroy all the works of Almighty God.

(d) Later in chapter 17:3 & 8 we are given further details of the meaning and importance of this beast.

5. The Beast from the Earth. 13:11-18

(a) We now review the authority and power of the beast from the Earth. This is the third and final beast within the unholy trinity and he will continue to attempt to overthrow the authority of Almighty God. The false prophet "had two horns like a lamb and spoke like a dragon", 13:11. His special description is that of a lamb and it would appear that he is attempting to claim the right to be the "Lamb of God" but his speech reveals that of a dragon. At first sight he appears to be as gentle as a lamb but this hides his real character of a dragon. His responsibility is to deceive all on earth to obey implicitly the demands of the Antichrist. The false prophet is also given the power to do "great signs" which will persuade the majority to worship the Antichrist. He will demand that an image of the beast (the Antichrist) must be erected and all living on the earth must worship this image. All who refuse will be executed. We see here now a radical change in several areas within the last three and a half years since the time that the rapture took place. At this stage the false prophet is given the authority to cause the image of the beast to become alive with the ability to breath and to speak. This is no mere ordinary idol, but one that has the ability to force each individual living upon earth to be obedient to the demands of Satan, the Antichrist and the false prophet.

(b) We come now to one of most debated verses in Scripture. The false prophet enforces a supreme law that every person living on the earth must receive an identity mark on their right hand or their forehead. Any that refuse to obey will be unable to buy or sell anything, and there will be no alternative method by which anybody will be able to purchase anything. All we know concerning any details of the "mark placed upon their right hand or forehead" is that the mark is "666". There have been many proposals concerning the meaning of this special mark and it is possible that the real secret may not be revealed until the actual time of the setting up of the image. However there are a few special aspects that we may be able to understand before that coming time.

(c) We are told quite clearly that the "name of the beast is a number" and it is only recently that numbers have supplanted the use of names in many areas such as banking, insurance, addresses, employment in large organisations, and many other systems. When we purchase our everyday goods, the majority of people pay for their purchases by using a credit or debit card.

This passage states quite clearly that one of the essential aspects of the Antichrist is that he will have complete control of all "buying and selling", 13:17. Until fairly recently any money transactions involving other countries were often very slow to organise, but today it is usually rapid and straight forward to transfer considerable values of money or goods rapidly from one country to another. The international systems for controlling or transferring money are now ready to be used for the future world dictator, although few appreciate the importance that the control of money will have in the future. There are those who believe we should dispense with all coinage and bank notes and rely entirely on computerised systems. As we look into God's Word we can now understand that this passage reveals to us that the control of all "buying and selling" is already in place waiting for the Antichrist to take over total control of all on earth at that time.

(d) Earlier we saw that many of the Jews accepted the rule of the Antichrist because he had built a temple to replace the one that was destroyed in AD 70 by the Romans. The Jews have always mourned the terrible loss of their temple and have always believed that in a coming day their temple would once again be in the place chosen by God where they would be able to worship Him. We refer now to the passage that we have already noted under "the interlude between the sixth and the seventh trumpets in Chapter 11:1-2" in which there is reference to the new temple being built in Jerusalem. At that time it would appear that the Jews believed that the Antichrist was a good benevolent leader because of the gift of the new temple. Once we reach the half-way of the reign of the Antichrist, he will reveal his true nature and make a final attempt to rule over all on this planet. All those who refuse to worship this image will be killed without mercy. It would appear that there will be two individual groups who are likely to rebel and refuse to worship the image. These will be the remnant of the Israelites and also the remnant of Ishmael (mainly Moslem) because they are the only large groups who are likely to refuse to worship idols.

Recently throughout the world in most of the individual countries there has been an explosive increase in the number of false religions. These have included idolatry, false teaching, Satanic worship and also the closing of many church buildings. This situation has already been noted under the introduction at the beginning of this book.

Summary: The first person of this unholy trinity is Satan himself (12:1-7), the second is the Antichrist (13:1-10), and the third and final person is usually referred to as the "false prophet", (13:11-18).

THIS IS NOW IN HEAVEN

6. **The Reward for Faithfulness for the 144,000 who were given a Special Responsibility. 14:1-5.**

John now has a special vision of the "Lamb of God". This is concerned with the reward given to the 144,000 for special responsibility and faithfulness referred to in reference 7:1-8. An important identification mark has been placed upon each of these faithful servants and this is "the Father's Name". They are also referred to as the "first fruits to God and to the Lamb". In contrast to this there are those on earth who will rebel against the living God and are willing to have the "mark of the beast" placed upon them, 13:15-17. All will have one or other identification. Names often had important meanings in scripture such as "at the Name of Jesus every knee should bow", Phil 2:10-11. Other references in Revelation are, "I will give him a white stone, and on the stone, a new name written which no one knows except him who receives it", 2:17. Also, "I will write on him My new name", 3:12.

THIS IS NOW ON THE EARTH

7.   The Absolutely Final Opportunity to Repent. 14:6-20

(a) The first angel proclaims the "everlasting gospel" upon every nation, tribe, tongue and people, 14:6-7. This is the final opportunity for any still remaining on the earth to repent. The message is "Fear God, and give glory to Him" which is the same message given to Adam, to Moses, and to all generations. As far as we can tell the Holy Spirit has been removed from the earth at the Rapture, see also 5:9-10. Examples in the Old Testament of those who "Feared God" are: Joseph, Moses, Daniel, Isaiah, Jeremiah, Ezekiel, etc.

(b) The second angel proclaims the "Fall of Babylon" which is in two stages, Religious and Political, 14:8. This is the commencement of the fall of Religious Babylon. See chapters 17 & 18 for more details of Babylon.

(c) The third angel proclaims a severe warning upon those who receive the "Mark of the Beast", 14:9-11. He warns of the serious result of ignoring this severe warning and the terrible result if they worship the Antichrist. "He will drink of the wine of the wrath of God". The choice for all is either the "Mark of God" (see 14:1) or the "Mark of the beast", God or Antichrist, God or Satan. All are warned that to worship the Antichrist will result in everlasting torment and not mere death.

(d) The faithful are blessed in martyrdom and this passage ends with the unbroken blessings for the faithful, 14:12-13.

(e) The preparation for the Day of Judgement, 14:14-16. The time of harvest has now come and the division between the "wheat and tares" is the first stage. See also Matt 13:37-43. The emphasis here is upon the "Son of Man" see also Dan 7:13-14.

(f) The final reaping is followed by judgement, 14:17-20. This is the reaping of the grapes of wrath in the "great winepress of the wrath of God". The "winepress was trampled outside the city and the blood poured for 1600 furlongs". This has been calculated to be equivalent to 200 miles. This would be equal to the distance from Dan to Beersheba which is representative to cover all of

Israel. The phrase "outside the city" reminds us of the location of Calvary.

THIS IS NOW IN HEAVEN

8.   The Preparation for the Bowl Judgements. 15:1-16:1.

(a) We are now given another great and marvellous sign in Heaven, 15:1-2. This consists of seven angels who have the seven final plagues ready to be used when God gives the order to commence the battle of Armageddon, see also chapter 16:16. There is a special blessing for those who have gained the victory "over the beast, and over his image, and over his mark and over the number of his name, which is 666." See chapter 13:11-18.

(b) This is followed by the "Song of Moses" and the "Song of the Lamb" who is the Lord Jesus Himself, 15:3-4. We are told that "All nations shall come and worship before you". We believe that the time is almost ready when everyone will acknowledge that Jesus Christ is Lord over all. It will be an amazing sight when every one of the world's great leaders of all types and all nations will bow before Him in worship and contrition.

(c) The Temple (the sanctuary or inner shrine) is opened in Heaven, 15:5-8. Coming out of the Holy Temple were seven angels each of which carried one of the seven bowls which contained the absolute final judgement upon all of those who had not repented of their sin.

There remains no more opportunity for repentance, only that of judgement.

H. THE SEVEN LAST PLAGUES AND FINAL JUDGEMENT. 16:1-18:24.

THIS IS NOW ON EARTH

1.   The comparison between the Trumpets and the Bowls (Vials)

The vials (or bowls) of God's wrath are punishments not warnings as the trumpets were, but there are many parallels between trumpets and bowls. The bowls are far worse than any other previous judgement. It is the final judgement before the return of the Lord Jesus to this earth in power and authority.   Below is a short comparison between the trumpets and the bowls.

2. Summary of Trumpets Judgements. (8:7 to 11:19). See also section F.

(a) Hail, fire and blood. A third of all trees and all grass destroyed, 8:7.

(b) A great fire is cast into the sea. A third of all the sea is changed into blood and a third of all creatures in the sea are killed. One third of all ships are also destroyed, 8:8-9.

(c) A great star falls from heaven resulting in a third of all rivers and springs becoming polluted. Many die as a result, 8:10-11.

(d) A third of the sun, the moon and the stars are totally damaged. A severe warning is also given regarding the last three trumpets, 8:12-13.

(e) The opening of the bottomless pit resulting in severe torment, 9:1-12.

(f) The angels from the Euphrates were now released to kill a third of mankind, 9:13-21.

(g) The Kingdom proclaimed and Jesus Christ now claims His right to be the King of kings and Lord of lords. The temple of God is opened in Heaven, 11:15-19.

3. Details of the Bowls of God's Wrath. 16:1-21.

This passage reveals the result of the wrath of Almighty God as the world that has rejected Him draws rapidly to the final judgement upon all those who have defied the commandments of Him. The main difference between the judgements of the bowls and that of the trumpets is that the judgements of the bowls are far worse, as we shall see.

(a) The first bowl is poured out upon earth. A loathsome sore appears upon those who had the "mark of the beast and who had worshipped his image." Here we have a clear connection between the worship of the beast and the severe penalty that Almighty God will pour upon all those who defy Him, 16:2

(b) The second bowl is poured out upon the sea. The sea is turned to blood and every living creature in the sea dies, 16:3

(c) The third bowl is poured out upon the rivers and springs on the earth and all water is changed to blood. This was because they had shed the blood of the saints and the prophets, and God now gives them their just due. There is a clear emphasis upon the fact that the Lord God Almighty is righteous and perfect in all of His judgements, 16:4-7.

(d) The forth bowl is poured out upon the sun. The heat of the sun was raised to give it the ability of pouring extreme pain upon all who refused to repent. This is not a cosmic accident but the righteous judgement of our Holy God upon those who have deliberately turned their back upon Him. Vast numbers are scorched by the intense heat but no one repented of their sin, instead they blasphemed the Name of God, 16:8-9.

(e) The fifth bowl is poured out upon earth and the result is darkness and severe torments over all, but they still did not repent. Rather than repenting they blasphemed the name of Almighty God, 16:10-11.

(f) The sixth bowl is poured out upon the River Euphrates. We have already seen the importance of the Euphrates under section "F", "5" and paragraph (g). The River Euphrates is now totally dried up in readiness to prepare the way for the kings of the East. This is the start of the last great battle of Armageddon and this is the only place in Scripture where the location of this final battle is given. It is also just one part of all the mass that will be gathered together because all of the armies throughout the whole world will be involved in this final battle. This great battle is not the result of the decision of world leaders, but that of the Lord Almighty Who gathers the nations to fight there. No man chooses either the time or the place of this battle. In addition to the huge armies that are gathered together there is now the additional situation of "the spirits of demons" who are adding to the terrible carnage that will be the result of battle. 16:12-16.

There are a number of references in the Old Testament to "Megiddo" which is the Old Testament location of "Armageddon". This was also the historical location of several ancient battles.

(g) Within the teaching of these seven bowls there is one verse which appears to be quite different from the remainder, 16:15.   This is the severe warning, "Behold, I am coming as a thief, blessed is he who watches and keeps his garments". Some would state that this is the Second Coming when all of those who are truly ready to meet their Lord are caught to be with Him for all time. This however does not fit in with the teaching of chapter 5:9-10, as well as several other verses. This state's quite clearly that "You, the Lord Jesus Christ, have redeemed us to God by your blood out of every tribe and tongue and people and nation. And we shall reign on the earth". This great coming event is the return of the Lord Jesus with His saints when He comes back to this earth as the King of kings, see 19:11-16.

(h) The seventh bowl is poured out into the air, 16:17-21. Is this because Satan was the "Prince of the power of the air"? (Eph 2:2). But he has already been cast down to earth in 12:7-9. Maybe this is concerned with aerial warfare? It is more likely to be something that will be revealed in the future of which we now have no knowledge. We must not speculate where we cannot fully understand. Even at the time of the seventh bowl, a part of the final crushing of Satan and his armies is that of "noises, thundering and lightening" which may be the result of some terrible storm much worse than we have ever visualised.

This circumstance is made far worse by having the most powerful earthquake that there has ever been in the history of the world. The prophecies in scripture have made it quite clear that severe earthquakes are an important aspect of prophecy. There are many today who are staggered at the increasing frequency of earthquakes as well as the increasing damage that they cause. A few years ago an entire National Geographical Magazine was dedicated to the situation relating from the increased problems concerning earthquakes. There is no doubt that this is one of the most important signs reminding us that the "Time of the end is drawing rapidly to a close". See Zech 14:4 which forecasts quite clearly that the Mount of Olives will be split in two parts on the Day that the Lord Jesus returns in power to this earth. Even islands and mountains will disappear totally. Our Lord gives us a clear warning that "If those days were not shortened ... no one would be left alive", Matt 24:21-22.

4. The Judgement of the Great Harlot. 17:1-18.

(a) Before we look closely at the "great harlot", it is essential that we understand the difference between each of the three false leaders who combine to complete the false trinity. Chapter 17 is concerned with Babylon as a false religious system. Chapter 18 is concerned with Babylon as a centre of governmental control, commerce, wealth, banking and a host of various systems and controls, all of which led to evil culture and moral decadence. We have then three beasts, all of whom are totally opposed to that of the Holy Trinity consisting of the Lord God, the Son and the Holy Spirit. These three beasts are now listed. The first is Satan, also known as the Dragon or the Devil, see also chapters 12:1-17 & 20:1-3. The second Beast who rose up out of the sea, had seven heads and ten horns. He was like a leopard, his feet were like the feet of a bear and his mouth like the mouth of a lion. He would be Satan's right hand leader and was instrumental in organising the vast armies in an attempt to control all who lived on this earth, see also 13:1-10. Finally there was the "Beast from the Earth" who had two horns like a lamb and spoke like the Dragon. He was given the authority to produce great signs which deceived those living on the earth. He was the one who made an image of the Beast and also commanded that all worship this image. He also demanded that none may buy or sell anything unless they have the "Mark of the beast" upon their right hand or upon their forehead, see also 13:11-18. You will note that the overall time of total control by the Dragon and his two evil associates is only very short.

(b) The great harlot is the one "who sat on many waters" and had considerable control over all the nations that were under the heel of Babylon. These included many that were involved in false religious systems which often had a considerable control over whole countries and even groups of countries, and we see that situation today. However, she did not have the authority herself but was controlled by the beast with the seven heads and ten horns who is the beast from the sea,13:1, who is also known as the Antichrist, 17:1-5. The titles given to the "scarlet woman" are: "Mystery, Babylon the great, the mother of harlots, and of the abominations of the earth". There is no doubt that this is an exceptionally evil being who desires to have complete control over all others. She was largely responsible for the final false religious system which also led to the martyrdom of many true saints.

(c) The power of religious control is shown in 17:6-8. This passage is concerned with the "scarlet woman" who is also called the "great harlot or whore". However we must be very careful and understand the clear difference between the authority of the "scarlet women" and that of "Second Beast". There are many who believe that she is the "Antichrist" but we have difficulty in accepting this for two reasons. Some of the names and titles are referred to as "a mystery". One important name is that of "Antichrist" which is found only in 1 John 2:18, 2:22, 4:3 and 2 John 7 and in no other references. It is very interesting that these references are all written by the Apostle John who was also chosen by God to write this book of Revelation.

We are told that the "woman was arrayed in purple and scarlet and adorned with gold and pearls". Only the richest and most powerful would be able to dress in this way, but this also emphasises the special dress for those who are leaders over false worship. Similar clothing is still used today in many religions.

(d) We are also told in verse nine that she had seven heads, and we are also told quite clearly that the interpretation of the "seven heads" represents "seven mountains or hills", 17:9. This can only refer to Rome. Although there are other cities built on seven hills, we must always understand that Rome was the last of the four great kingdoms permitted by God (see Daniel 2:36-45). Also, Rome has claimed the authority of being the centre for so-called Christianity for approximately 2000 years.

It is also very significant that recently there has been an attempt to merge the majority of different religions into one, which shows us without any doubt whatever that we are approaching the "last days". It is now nothing unusual to see leaders of various false faiths sharing so-called worship with others having a vastly different teaching.   One aspect of vital significance in understanding what the Bible teaches us concerning the future nations is the rapidly increasing power of Islam. Not only are they rapidly increasing their influence throughout the whole world, but there are many who believe that such a movement would be for the good of all. Without any doubt this is now preparing the way for the final judgement of those who refuse to accept the claims of the Lord Jesus Christ. God's word states that, "They will also make war with the Lamb, and the Lamb will overcome them, for He is Lord of lords and King of kings". The completion of this firm promise is reviewed in the next section "I" in chapter 19.

(e) We are also informed that there will be another seven kings but that five of these will have fallen by this stage leaving only two to come at this period of time. One will already be here during this series of final events but the last one is yet to come, 17:10. During these absolutely final days before the Lord returns in power, ten kings will be given special authority to reign with the beast but this will be for only one hour, 17:11-14. These will all be "one mind" therefore there will be total unity and agreement because they will give "their power and authority unto the beast". This also indicates that all of the world's individual religions will merge together and form one world-wide false faith under the total control of the beast. The "scarlet woman" will also be involved in this but instead of a reward for this responsibility, the beast will "hate the harlot and make her desolate" see 17:16. It is only recently that we have seen the merging together of many of the leading false religious groups.

(f) Babylon, that great city, is now drawing rapidly to its final judgement as we shall see in the next section, 17:18 & 18:2-3. The beast who now has the authority to destroy the "scarlet woman" believes that he is now able to rule the entire earth. What he does not understand is that all the authority that he now has, is only because it is by the permission of Almighty God Himself. In 17:17 we read, "For God has put it into their hearts to fulfil His purpose, to be of one mind, and to give their kingdom to the beast, until the words of God are fulfilled". The Lord God will have the final control over all. No others will have any influence whatever upon the events of these last times.

5.   The fall of Babylon. Chapter 18.

(a) An extremely powerful angel is given the special responsibility of announcing the downfall of Babylon. In our study we have seen a gradual climax concerning the power and authority of Babylon. By this final time all the false religions will have been taken over by the beast and all aspects will be merged into one controlling system. Babylon itself will be controlled by demons, foul spirits and vicious scavenging birds. All nations will have drunk of the wrath of her fornication and the merchants will become tremendously rich, 18:1-3.

We saw under chapter 17 section (b), that the main emphasis of the importance of Babylon is that they were using religion to control the nations. The events in chapter 18 are somewhat different because they are controlling the nations by the use of demonism, 18:2, fornication, riches and luxury, 18:3. Babylon is now a centre of commerce, wealth, banking, finance, agriculture, industry, government, culture and moral decadence, and anything else that will give the beast an evil control over all.

(b) We also see that Almighty God will from this time issue the absolute last opportunity to repent and return to a loving Holy God, 18:4. The Antichrist will do all in his power to prevent any from seeking the salvation that is now being offered. He will see no need of having any false religion as he will set himself up to be the only god, but this claim will be very short lived.

(c) This is one of the saddest portions of scripture because for thousands of years the Lord God continually pleaded with those who had refused His loving kindness. In addition to this He had sent His Only Son, the Lord Jesus Christ, to pay the penalty of our sin on the Cross of Calvary. Despite this there are still many who have turned their back upon the only One that is able to give them a totally new life. No one may continually defy the Almighty Creator of all without eventually facing the terrible consequences, 18:5-8. We are told clearly in 18:5 that "God has remembered her iniquities".

(d) We come now to the result of the defeat of Babylon, 18:9-24. As we noted in 17:5, "Babylon" and the "mother of harlots" are interwoven together as a unit. Throughout the teaching concerning Babylon it is usually referred to as "she" indicating that this is the same harlot who is involved with evil. In God's sight the evil of Babylon is so vile that they are given a terrible penalty which is before the judgement meted out when Jesus Christ returns in glory to this earth. This section from 18:9-20 gives important details concerning the terrible results of defying our Holy Lord God.

(i)   The great city of Babylon took many hundreds of years
       to complete but it only took one hour for God to destroy
       it utterly, 18:9-19.

(ii)   The kings of the earth were far more concerned with
       their loss of luxurious living than having any desire to be
       right with a Holy God. They were on the verge of having
       to face the Lord God Himself and give an account on
       their totally wasted lives, but they are still only concerned
       with their material losses that are now lost for all eternity.

(iii) One particular phrase sums up the evil within their
       satanic system and this is that the "bodies and the souls
       of men" are treated merely as merchandise, to be sold
       as slaves with no freedom whatever, 18:13. When they
       are of no use to their owners they will be killed off. The
       Antichrist is able to influence men by using the occult so
       that they sell their souls to Satan. We have already
       noted that all those living on earth must have the Mark
       of the Beast upon them or be unable to buy or sell. The
       unholy trinity consisting of Satan, the beast and the false
       prophet will have total control over all those who are
       now the only inhabitants of the earth. The whore who
       was totally evil will soon be killed as she will be the first to
       meet the judgement of Almighty God, 19:2.

(e)   There is a clear difference between those who were
       faithfully willing to trust and obey the Lord Jesus Christ
       and those who rejected His claims and refused to
       accept the new life that only He can give.   This
       difference is clearly understood by comparing 18:19-20.

Despite all the many warnings that were given to those involved with Babylon, there was clearly no attempt to return to the God they had despised. Their only interest was that they had lost all their wealth and all that Babylon could offer. By contrast those who are truly saved are given true rejoicing in Heaven. Not only was Babylon totally destroyed but God's Word makes it quite clear that it will never be rebuilt. This is the commencement of the defeat of Satan and all that he had planned. God now begins to repay all those who have defied Him, the time of final reckoning will now begin, 18:21-24.

6.   A Brief History of Man's Rebellion against our Loving and Holy God.

(a) The first rebellion against Almighty God was that of Adam and Eve in the Garden of Eden. The result of this was that sin entered the world leading eventually to the death of all mankind. In those early days the majority of each of the population lived to between eight hundred and nine hundred years, see Genesis chapters 2-5.

(b) The second rebellion is listed in Genesis 6:1-8. It is recorded that "the Lord was sorry that He had made man on the earth, and He was grieved in His heart". It is well known that "only Noah found grace in the eyes of the Lord" and because of this only Noah and his close family were saved from total drowning in the resultant flood. The only other living creatures saved from total destruction were a small selection of each of the animals, birds, insects, and others. When the flood eventually receded, God made a promise that never again would He destroy the earth in this way, Gen 8:21-22. Some may ask "what about the coming judgement that is forecast in the Book of Revelation?" The answer is absolutely clear! We read in Revelation 21:1 that "I saw a new heaven and new earth for the first heaven and the first earth were passed away".

(c) The next rebellion against Almighty God was the building of the Tower of Babel, Gen 11:1-9. Throughout the Old Testament the name of Babel is used interchangeably with that of Babylon. Babylon was founded by Nimrod, Gen 10:9-12 & Micah 5:6. They rebelled against God by building the "Tower of Babel", and they have always stood for enmity with God. Babylon was also the first system of Astrology, see also Isaiah 47:12-13 & Dan 2:2, "Astrologers, Magicians and Chaldeans" all tracing their roots back to Babel. Later the religions of Babylon were absorbed by Persia, Greece and then Rome. These "traditions" were later partly absorbed into the "Holy Roman Empire" which replaced pagan Rome. Associated with Papal Rome, the complete "united" false multi-faith religious system evolved with all forms of astrology and Satanic worship with the false prophet as its head.

(d) It is believed that all of the early false gods were a direct result of the influence of Babylon. Ancient legend states that Nimrod was born supernaturally from his wife, and also that carvings and idols of them as "mother and son" were an object of worship. It is claimed that from these the following have developed: Ashtaroth & Tammuz (Phoecia); Isis & Horus (Egypt); Aphrodite & Eros (Greece); Venus & Cupid (Rome); Nimrod himself has been identified with Bacchus, Tammuz and Adonis. His wife has been identified with Semvanis, Cybele, Aphrodite & Venus.

7. **Before we move to a study of the next title let us remind ourselves once again of the systematic development that runs throughout almost all of the Book of Revelation starting with chapter 4.**

This same pattern continues unbroken until verse 11 of the last chapter. God Himself has designed the development of this wonderful prophecy, therefore we need to read it, to study it and to appreciate the essential teaching that is all there for our guidance and blessing. For some it may be helpful to go back to the beginning of our study: "A. Setting the basis for our study" and "Section 8: The importance of the order of events", at the beginning of this review of the Book of Revelation.

I. THE DAY OF THE LORD WHEN ALL WRONGS WILL BE RIGHTED.

THIS EVENT NOW STARTS IN HEAVEN BUT IS RAPIDLY CONCERNED WITH CHRIST RETURNING TO THIS EARTH FOR THE FIRST TIME SINCE HIS DEATH AND RESURRECTION.

1. The preparation for the return of the Lord. 19:1-10.

(a) The choice between one of two responses, Praise or Rebellion. We have then the faithful multitude in Heaven worshipping their Saviour and Lord. "Alleluia! Salvation and glory and honour and power belong to the Lord our God", 19:1. The only alternative is "The great harlot who has corrupted the earth with her fornication", 19:2.

(b) There is also the choice between the two suppers. There is rejoicing by the faithful saints compared with defeat and judgment for those who defied the Almighty Holy God. The two alternatives are clearly listed. It will be either the "Marriage supper of the Lamb" for those who have accepted the new life of Christ, 19:7-9, with the only alternative being severe judgement upon those who were corrupted by the great harlot. There is also the terrible feast for the birds of prey which we will see later, 19:17-18.

(c) Already "God has judged the great harlot who corrupted the earth with her evil ways, and she is now suffering beyond anything that we may understand". She was the first of the evil leaders to be judged by God Himself. There will be no need to wait until the Great White Throne is set up because the Lord God has already uttered the final condemnation. "He has avenged on her the blood of His servants shed by her", 19:2-4. This is also the final punishment of all who have defied the warning given by the Lord God. This will soon be revealed.

(d) The marriage supper of the Lamb is one of the most important events that will ever occur. This event reveals the special bond between the Saviour and His faithful followers. It is not merely something of interest but it reveals the extreme love that our Lord promises to all of those who are truly His. "He is the head of the body, the church, who is the beginning, the firstborn from the dead, that in all things He might have the pre-eminence", Col 1:18. That will be a great day when our Lord shares with us that unique marriage supper. Just before His crucifixion, our Lord instituted "His special Supper" but He also said "I will not drink of the fruits of the vine until I drink it new with you in My Father's kingdom", Matt 26:26-29. He is still waiting for that special time. That will indeed be a unique meal, 19:5-10.

Also for other important teaching concerning the Wedding Ceremony see Matt 25:1-13. This challenges us to be sure that we are ready to meet our coming Saviour.

The Wedding Dress is made from "pure white linen" which is the "Righteousness of the Saints", 19:8. This is identical to those returning with their Lord, 19:14. Who are those invited to this Feast? We are not told exactly who these are. Perhaps the Old Testament saints or the Tribulation saints? We do know that our Lord Himself stated that "Other sheep I have which are not of this fold; them also I must bring, and they will hear My Voice and there will be one flock and one Shepherd". We have then a clear statement that there are other sheep but we are not given any clear details of who they are. Therefore we must never assume anything that is not clearly set out in Scripture.

The Bride is distinguished from Israel the unfaithful wife of Jehovah, who is now restored and will be redeemed at the Millennium. See Psalm 45:6-8; Is 62:3-5; Jer 31:3-6. These verses state that Israel is the wife of Jehovah who will be restored to her full position in the latter days.

2.   The return of the Lord Jesus Christ in power. 19:11-16.

The purpose of His return covers a number of different vital events and we need to understand God's overall plan for all concerned.

(a) The first important situation is to understand and accept the authority that is bestowed upon the One Who alone is worthy to reign. Heaven is opened and the Lord Jesus Christ prepares to return to earth for the first time since His ascension approximately two thousand years ago.

We have no doubt concerning His authority because we are given His special titles which are "Faithful and True", 19:11, "The Word of God" 19:13, and "King of kings and Lord of lords", 19:16. In addition to this, He was given "a name written that no one knew except Himself", 19:12.

(b) The "Armies in Heaven" are clearly those who have been chosen by God for the very special purpose of defeating the evil power of Satan. The Leader of this army is the Lord Jesus Christ Himself. We are told that "In righteousness He judges and makes war", 19:11. Also the armies in Heaven are preparing to accompany their Leader and Saviour on His return to this earth. It is particularly important that the special clothing made for those who accompany their Lord on His return to this earth is identical to that worn by those who were worthy to be invited to the Marriage supper of the Lamb. These two events are then interwoven one to the other and this would indicate that these two unique events are concerned with the same group of God's faithful servants, 19:11 & 14. Another very important teaching is also the fact that this is the first time that the true church has been mentioned since they were redeemed and were now in heaven, 5:9-10.

(c) He comes as the Judge of all Mankind, "He Himself will rule all nations", 19:15. See also "The Father judges no one, but has committed all judgement to the Son", John 5:22-23, 27 & 30; Acts 10:42, 17:31; Rom 2:16.

(d) A little earlier during the pouring out of the bowls of

God's wrath (see reference 16:15) those still awaiting the coming of their Lord were encouraged by the promise, "Lo I come as a thief". That promise is now being fulfilled. It will be totally unexpected by those who have followed Satan and his leaders.

(e) Some believe that this coming is synonymous with the Rapture but we need to appreciate what the Bible teaches concerning this. A careful study of the teaching of God's plan will reveal that there is a clear distinction between the "Rapture" and the "Day of the Lord". For details of the Rapture we turn to reference 5:9-10, where we are told quite clearly that Jesus Christ is in Heaven together with all of those who have been redeemed by the Blood of Christ. Immediately after His resurrection, our Lord revealed Himself only to those who had been faithful to Him. Just as He was ascending into Heaven, two special men from Heaven gave His disciples a most important promise, which was that "This same Jesus, who was taken into Heaven, will come in like manner as you have seen Him go into Heaven", Acts 1:11. There is no mention of these returning back to this earth at this stage. Events must follow what God has already planned.

(f) The rapture of the Saints has already taken place so this must be the "Day of the Lord", when the Lord returns for His own who have repented of their sin and have been faithful to their Lord despite terrible persecution. Another vital fact is that following the systematic teaching as taught from Revelation chapter 4:1 through to 22:17, there is an unbroken development of God's plan, leaving us in no doubt regarding God's purposes for His own people. The special promise at the Ascension (Acts 1:11) is unique because we are told that "This same Jesus who was taken from you into Heaven, will come in like manner as you have seen Him go". This promise states clearly that this refers to the same Person, the Lord Jesus Himself, Who will be in the same place, which will be "The Mount of Olives", Zech 14:4-8. At that time the disciples asked if He was about to restore the kingdom (Acts 1:6), and He now comes to do just that. There is also an additional confirmation of this great event which is given in Zechariah chapter 14. This lists many parallels with God's final judgement upon the many who have defied the commands of Almighty God.

(g) He is clothed with a robe that is dipped in Blood. See 19:13-14 together with Isaiah 63:1-6, which reminds us of the cost of our salvation. He is accompanied by His saints all dressed identically in the same robes as the Bride – pure, clean, white linen.

(h) We now approach the actual future time when our Lord returns to this earth for the first time since His ascension, 19:11-16. This time everything will be vastly different as He will come as the "King of kings and the Lord of lords", 19:16. With Him will be "the armies of Heaven", 19:14. These will include all who have been faithful to their Lord and Saviour. The special armies that will accompany the return of the Lord Jesus will all have one great advantage compared with the enemy, they will all have total immunity from anything that Satan can possibly produce. Our Lord promises that "Over such the second death has no power", 20:6. "Oh death where is your sting, O grave? O Hades where is your victory? The sting of death is sin, and the strength of sin is the law. But thanks be to God, who gives us the victory through our Lord Jesus Christ", 1 Cor 15: 55-58.

3. The setting up of His Kingdom and the final stage of Armageddon. 19:17-20:3

(a) Preparation for the coming slaughter of the followers of the Antichrist. The name Armageddon is listed only in 16:16. This is given to the hill and valley of Megiddo, west of the Jordan in the Plain of Jezreel between Samaria and Galilee. This is also called the Valley of Jehoshaphat in Joel 3:12.

(b) The beast and the kings of the earth gather together with their vast armies in a false attempt to defeat totally the armies of the King of kings. This is the final attempt by the Antichrist and his followers to establish their evil kingdom. This will lead to the total defeat of their evil armies.

(c) The two rewards. The first reward is that given to the only One who was able to accept such a great position of authority, the Lord Jesus Himself. "His eyes were a flame of fire, and on His head were many crowns. And His name is called the Word of God", 19:12-13. This reminds us of the special title given to our Lord in the introduction of John's gospel.

(d) The other reward was completely the opposite, as it was one of retribution and referred to those who were totally opposed to all that God required of them. These were in every way deserving the punishment that Almighty God has meted out to them. Their reward was that, "The beast and the false prophet and those who worshipped his image were cast alive into the lake of fire, burning with brimstone", 19:20-21. Throughout all of our life there are only two alternatives, there is no middle course. Either we accept the salvation that the Lord Jesus offers us and allow Him to cleanse us from sin and by His strength to live a life that is honouring to Almighty God in all that we do. The only alternative is to ignore the One Who died for us and to live only for ourselves and ignore His sacrifice on Calvary. We must choose either a life spent for God or a life without God; an eternity with God or an eternity without Him in Hell.

(e) The last great battle leading up to the defeat of the beast and the false prophet now takes place. These two enemies of God were captured and cast alive into the lake of fire, as there is no need to wait till the setting up of the Great White Throne, 19:17-21. There will also be others included in the remnant of the vast army from the East who have defied the earlier attempts to defeat the purposes of Almighty God. See earlier 9:13-18 & 16:12-16.

(f) Satan, the Dragon, that serpent of old, who is also referred to as the Devil, is bound for 1000 years, 20:3. The timing of this situation coincides with the Millennium Reign, and is dealt with under paragraph 5 below.

4.   A review of the resurrections in the last days.

There are several clearly defined resurrections that are shown in the book of Revelation. These have been drawn together into one paragraph so that we can remember many who have been faithful to their Lord and Saviour.

The first of these is our Lord Himself as shown in 4:1 to 5:14. Without His death, His resurrection and His new life in Heaven there would be no future for any of us. Throughout scripture there are several references to those who have been chosen of God for a special responsibility. This teaches us that Almighty God has the power over both life and death for various special reasons.

The Rapture will consist of all those who have accepted Him as their Saviour and Lord including those who have died and those who are still alive, see 5:9-10. The second group will be those who have come faithfully through the Tribulation, see 20:4-6.

In addition to these there are several chosen saints who were given a special responsibility in those last days. These include the apostle John who was given the task of committing this special Book into a readable form so that we are able to read what Almighty God has to teach us concerning the final days, 1:9-20. We then have the two witnesses, 11:1-14, and the 144,000 who were redeemed from the earth, 14:1-5.

Finally we have the resurrection of all those who have rejected the salvation that the Lord Jesus offered to all. This event will not be until the completion of the one thousand year millennium; and also the crushing of the final Satanic rebellion, 20:11.

5. The Millenium Reign. 20:4-6.

(a) This is a special situation unlike anything that has occurred since the creation of the world and all who have lived on it. There are only three verses in the Book of Revelation that reveal the purpose of this special situation, which is in order that those who have been truly faithful to the Lord Jesus will reign with Him for one thousand years, 20:4.

(b) Those who have already died without repentance for their sins will remain awaiting judgement, 20:5 & 11.

(c) The final promise is that those who are faithful to their Lord will never have to face death ever again. They will reign with their Lord for a thousand years on this earth but as we will see in chapter 21, this is still only the beginning of even greater blessings, 20:6.

(d) There is much throughout God's Word that gives us further details concerning these very last days on earth so we will remind ourselves of all the many amazing situations that our Lord has promised us.

(i) All war will be a thing of the past. "Nation will not take up sword against nation nor will they train for war any more", Is 2:1-4.

(ii)   "The Lord will be King over the whole earth", Zech 14:9
        & 21.

(iii)   The land also will be regenerated and will "become like
        the Garden of Eden", Ez 36:24-38, creation will be
        restored as it was before the fall. The "wolf and the
        lamb", the "leopard and the young goat", the "lion and
        the calf", the "cow and the bear" and the "baby and
        the cobra" will all live together in complete harmony. All
        nature (even the insects) shall be changed, "They will
        not hurt nor destroy in all of My Holy mountain", Isaiah
        11:9 & 65:25.

(iv)   The plant kingdom will also be regenerated, because
        there will be no more nettles, briars, thorns, or even plant
        allergies, Is 30:23-24 & 35:1-2 & 6-7, 41:18-20 & 51:3. Trees
        and plants of all types will all grow freely on land that
        was previously a wilderness; and the wilderness and the
        desert becoming like the Garden of Eden.

(v)   The people who have survived Armageddon will have
        improved physical conditions and an extended life
        span, Is 35:3-6. We are also told that, "For as it is for the
        days of a tree, so shall it be for My people", Is 65:22. In
        addition to this, there is another vital reference in the
        prophecy of Isaiah that also confirms the fact that
        ordinary people will live much longer than they do
        today. The fact that this is recorded in the book of Isaiah
        is very important. The Bible records that Methuselah
        lived to be almost a thousand years old, Gen, 5:25-27,
        and if we read through the list of those who lived during

that time we see that the majority lived for longer than any other group of people since then, Gen 5:1-32.

(vi) Another aspect of those future times is the promise that "The days are coming, declares the LORD, when ... I will bring back My exiled people Israel ... I will plant Israel in their own land, never again to be uprooted from the land I have given them", Amos 9:11-15. "You shall know that I am the LORD, when I have ... put my Spirit in you and you shall live, and I shall place you in your own land", Ez 37:1-14. "They shall not hurt nor destroy in all My Holy mountain, says the Lord", Is 65:25. If we do not accept all of these remarkable promises we will be guilty of "taking away" some of God's Word, 22:18-19.

(e) There is much debate by some as to whether this is a literal 1000 years but the fact that the thousand years is stated six times in the short list of chapter twenty is exceptionally significant. 20: 2, 3, 4, 5, 6 & 7. The overall time of both the Millennium Reign and the overall time of the binding of Satan is also one thousand years making the two identical.

(f) A brief summary of the rapid situation leading to the final Judgement. At the final return of the Lord Jesus in power we read that the armies attacking Jerusalem will be destroyed and the Antichrist and the False Prophet will be cast into the "Lake of Fire", 19:11-20:3. But Satan himself will be "bound for a thousand years" while the Lord Jesus, the Messiah will rule the world. Following this reign, Satan will be released and will make his absolute final bid for overthrowing the authority of God, but he will rapidly meet with his judgement.

6.   The Final Satanic Rebellion. 20:7-10.

(a) After one thousand years of perfect peace throughout the world, the restraining hand of Almighty God will be removed for a short time and Satan will be released from his place of torment. Once again we see the emphasis placed upon the completion of the one thousand years, 20:7.   This final rebellion will be because God now demonstrates His authority over all who have rejected Him. We come therefore to the very last rebellion ever to be permitted by our Loving Holy Almighty God. He alone has the authority to control Satan to be released onto this earth for one final terrible attempt to reveal to all just how evil he really is. Parallel with this, only He, the Great Creator of all has the authority to mete out true and just punishments for those who have defied Him. Throughout the Book of Revelation Satan is also known as the Devil, the Dragon and the serpent of old. We are not told in the book of Revelation how long this war will take, but it would appear that this special final event will have a rapid conclusion.

(b) The emphasis upon "Gog and Magog" is also seen in Ezekiel chapters 38 and 39 and it is clearly concerned with the same future event, see 20:8. There are also a number of countries listed in Ezekiel which include Persia, Ethiopia and Libya that appear to be approximately in the same areas as those known today.

Some of the remaining countries are not clearly recognised at present.

(c) Not only do we see that Satan will be released from his prison but parallel with this there will be an uprising from a vast number of those who seek to destroy all that is pure and holy. They believe that Satan together with his vast armies will be able to defeat Almighty God. They have learned nothing from the huge defeats detailed earlier in chapters, 17:7-18; 18:1-24; 19:17-21 and 20:1-3.

(d) The final defeat will be upon all of those who have refused to accept the claims of a Holy Almighty God.

(e) Satan together with all of his followers will attempt one final rebellion but are totally defeated and they are cast into the lake of fire. From this there is no escape whatever but "they will be tormented day and night forever and ever", 20:9-10. Although this final rebellion will not occur until the completion of the Millennial reign of Christ, it is really a direct follow on from Armageddon.

(f) Throughout the book of Revelation there is constant reference to the importance of eternity. The phrase "forever and ever", emphasises God's Eternal Nature. The same Greek words are often used throughout Revelation, see 1:6 & 18, 4:9-10, 5:13-14, 7:12, 10:6, 11:15, 15:7 & Gal 1:3-5. There are also those who cannot accept that the penalty of defying a righteous God is also unending. Some would read into the phrase "the second death" in 20:14 & 21:8, as merely annihilation but the Bible makes it quite clear that this is not so. In 20:10 we read that those guilty of defying the Almighty God will be "tormented day and night forever and ever". This is the eventual cost to all who reject God's way of salvation. There is also a very similar statement in 14:10-11. See also 2 Thess 1:7-9.

7.   The final Judgement of all those who have not accepted the Lord Jesus Christ as their Saviour. 20:11-15

(a) The Great White Throne is the final judgement and refers to all those who lived and died without accepting the claims of the Lord Jesus Christ. The basis for all who are arrayed before this final place of judgement is what God has recorded concerning the lives of every individual.

(b) There are two essential, vastly different Books that are listed in the Book of Revelation. The first of these is concerned with the severe judgement based upon the true record that God has made for everyone who has ever lived upon this earth and has not accepted salvation. We are told that "the dead small and great are standing before Almighty God. ... And they were judged each one according to his works", 20:11-12.

(c) The final judgement concerning these "books" is the unique "Book of Life". This is a special list of those whose name is written in the Book of Life. These have not been added to this list because of any special holiness on their part, but because each has come to the Cross, confessing their sins and claiming the new Life that the Lord Jesus is willing to give to all those who have sincerely trusted Him.

(d) Why was this Book of Life written by the commandment of Almighty God? It was to draw our attention to the seriousness and urgency of the vital fact that this world has a very limited "use-by-date"! God will eventually destroy this earth, on which we now live, see 21:1. Each one of us is familiar with the "use-by-date" that is associated with many of the goods that we purchase. Some we accept and others are ignored. But here we have something that is vastly of more value than anything else that we can purchase, or make, or borrow, or rent, or steal. God Himself reminds each of us that a day is coming when all who have lived on this earth must give an account of how they have spent the life that He has given us. This is the challenge which is demonstrated in these few verses that we are reading at this very time. Be wise and read, study and understand the tremendous importance of these verses in 20:11-15 once again. Consider the seriousness of ignoring these verses which Almighty God has given us which will influence where we spend an unbroken eternity.

J. THE FINAL CONSUMATION AND ETERNITY.
THE NEW HEAVENS AND THE NEW EARTH. 21:1-22:21.

1.   The redeemed in the new Heaven. 21:1-8.

(a) Everything will be radically changed. There will be a
new earth and a new heaven, the existing heaven and
earth are to be destroyed, 21:1. There may be some
confusion concerning the situation that there will be a
"new heaven" because in the Bible there are three quite
separate heavens. This is dealt with under, "A. Setting the
basis for our study", see paragraph "10: The Importance
of the Location of Heaven in each Prophecy". It would
appear that the destruction of heaven and earth would
apply only to the heaven and earth which had been
damaged by their contact with sin.

(b) Also there will be no more sea. Throughout history the
sea and the oceans have always been important
barriers between nations, there will now no longer be
any need for such barriers, 21:1. This does not mean that
there will be no more flowing water such as rivers, see in
chapter 22:1-2.

(c) Throughout the Bible there are various promises that
Jerusalem was a special place chosen by God for the
purpose of worshiping the One True God. We now have
another firm promise that there is to be the new holy city,
"The New Jerusalem", 21:2. This future new city will be
"prepared as a bride adorned for her Husband". In the
epistle to the Hebrews there are several passages

concerning this special promise. We are told that Abraham "waited for the city which had foundations whose builder and maker is God", Heb 11:9-10. There were others of whom it was stated that "God is not ashamed to be called God, for He had prepared a city for them" Heb 11:16. See also Heb 12:18-24.

(d) We have the firm promise that "God Himself will be with them and be their God". There will be no more death, nor sorrow, nor crying, and no more pain because the former things have passed away. Everything will be new! 21:3-5.

(e) As we draw to the completion of this study, we are reminded of the commencement of this unique work in that the claim of Almighty God is unchanged from chapter 1 to our present position. This is demonstrated by the text, "I am the Alpha and Omega, the Beginning and the End", 1:8. We have an identical claim in chapter 21:6. There is one vital difference between these two verses and this is that in verse 1:8 we look forward to the promise of His coming which we are still doing. In verse 21:6 we have glorious news that "It is done!" Nothing can now be added or changed in any way, the work of Calvary is now totally complete.

We also have an amazing promise for those who "overcome" as they will "inherit all things" and are also given the promise that "I will be his God and he shall be My son", 21:6-7.

(f)   For all of those who have not at this stage accepted the Salvation that the Lord Jesus Christ offers freely, there is an urgent need for them to appreciate that the day of opportunity is rapidly drawing to a final close. We are also given a list of the terrible sins that are so prevalent today, many of which are not considered to be wrong by the majority. This list is not made by mere humans but by God Himself as seen in 21:8.   Therefore this list is the standard that is set by a Holy God; it is not made by mere men. This contains nothing new. Throughout the Bible there are many other warnings listing these same sins and warning of the terrible results of ignoring God's commandments. These then are the actions that cannot be tolerated by a Holy God: being cowardly, unbelieving, abominable, murderous, sexually immoral, sorceress, idolatrous or lying.   Are we on that list?

If we have not already done so, we need to come before the Lord God and repent of our sin before it is too late and we lose the new life He offers. This book of Revelation was never intended to be of mere interest or debate, but it is God's absolutely final warning to all upon this earth, 21:8.

2.   The New Jerusalem. 21:9-27

(a) One of the seven angels who had the seven last plagues (see 15:1) now has a special responsibility, that of introducing the "Bride of Christ" (see also 19:7-9). This passage clearly associates the Bride of Christ with the New Jerusalem, 21:9.

(b) John is now shown the "Holy Jerusalem descending out of Heaven". Heaven in this instant refers to the abode of God, having the glory of God. In 21:12 we are told that there are twelve gates in this Holy Jerusalem each of which has the name of one of the tribes of the children of Israel. The twelve foundations of the New Jerusalem are given the names of the twelve apostles. We see here the final joining together of the Old and the New Covenants, 21:10-14.

(c) Details are now given of the new city itself and as one would expect, it is vastly different from any city that we know. We are told that its length, its breath and its height are equal. The basic size of the city is given as twelve thousand furlongs so a reasonable approximation is about 1,380 miles cubed. In addition to this, there will be twelve gates but we are not told the purpose of these gates so we must not try to read into this something that we are not given. We have already noted that the New Jerusalem is vastly different from our present concept of a city. We now see the amazing variety of materials that are used for the building of the New Jerusalem, which include vast amounts of pure gold, very large pearls and a whole range of precious stones, 21:15-21.

(d) There is no need for a temple in Heaven because the "Lord God Almighty and the Lamb of God are their temple". Also there is "no need of the sun or the moon because the glory of God and of the Lamb is their light. All of those who are saved shall walk in its light". There is much that we cannot understand now concerning the beauty and the greatness of the many amazing blessings that our God has planned for us, 21:22-24.

(e) "The gates will never be closed. There will never be any night there ... They shall bring their glory and honour into it", 21:25-26.

(f) We are reminded once again that "only those whose names are written in the Lamb's Book of Life" are permitted to enter the New Jerusalem, 21:27.

3. The River Of Life. 22:1-5.

(a) We come now to the final promises of the future that the Lord has prepared for all those who have accepted the claims that are revealed throughout this wonderful Book of Revelation. The apostle is first of all shown the "Water of Life proceeding from the throne of God and of the Lamb". From this River of Life comes the "Tree of Life" yielding twelve special fruits, 22:1-2.

(b) There shall be no more curse, all evil will be a thing of the past. God Himself with His Son the Lamb will be with all those who truly love Him. We are told that "His servants shall serve Him" which indicates that He has already planned some special responsibility for all of those who are truly His. Each one of us who has truly accepted Him as our Saviour and Lord will be with Him in Heaven. We will bear His Name upon our forehead. This indicates a special relationship with Him in glory. We have seen earlier that Satan always tries to mimic the special things that God has already done, and in 13:17 he introduces the "mark of the beast" which all are commanded to obey. Satan's mark will lead to terrible judgement, but for all of those who are worthy to receive the Name of their Saviour upon their forehead it will bring blessings beyond compare. The very final promise is that all those who have been faithful and are truly His, "shall reign with Him forever and ever", 22:3-5.

K. THE FINAL WARNINGS AND PROMISES. 22:6-21.

(a) We now have conformation from God that all of the
words of this special book will soon be taking place. This
is coupled with the special promise given by the Lord
Himself, "Behold I come quickly! Blessed is he who keeps
the words of the prophecy of this book", 22:6-7. This
book started with a similar promise, see 1:3.

(b) For the second time the Apostle John (see 19:10) is so
overawed that he needed to be reminded that no
matter how special any of God's servants are at that
time, only God Himself is worthy of worship, 22:8-9.

(c) The time is coming when the entire population both
present and past will be clearly divided into those who
have accepted the Salvation offered by the Lord God
and those who have rejected it. Whatever our final
situation it can now never be changed for all eternity,
22:10-11.

(d) We have this severe warning in Galatians 6:7-8, "Do not
be deceived, God is not mocked, for whatever a man
shall sow, that shall he also reap. For he who sows to this
flesh will of the flesh reap corruption, but he who sows to
the Spirit will of the Spirit reap everlasting life". 22:10-11
in our study makes this absolutely clear that there is
coming a day when God's offer of salvation with be
withdrawn and there will no longer be any opportunity
to accept God's offer of a new life. At present we still

have the opportunity to turn to God in true repentance. If we have not already done so we must urgently seize this opportunity before it is too late. God's way offers only two alternatives. The first is to come to Him and to claim that cleansing from sin and to receive that new life that only He can give. The terrible alternative is to turn our back on Him and reject the new life that He offers. The choices are very clear and these are life or death, Heaven or Hell, spiritual growth or degeneration. There are no other alternatives whatever. We do not know when that day will dawn and there will be no further opportunities of salvation. For many this will be a day of supreme anguish and severe regret, but it will be too late.

At present we still have the opportunity to turn to God in true repentance, and if we have not already done so we must urgently seize this opportunity before it is too late. God's way is for us to accept His way of salvation, and to make us worthy of the cost of Calvary. The only other alternative is to reject the love of the Only One Who truly loves us, and if so, there will be no further possibility of salvation, 22:10-11.

(e) The very last reminder that the Day of the Lord will soon be here is now given. Our Lord once again reminds us that "He is the Alpha and the Omega, the Beginning and the End, the First and the Last", 22:13. This same title is also used twice in chapters 1:8 & 1:11 of Revelation indicating that this is an extremely special title.

(f) A final reminder and warning to those who will be "outside" the presence of the peace of God, 22:15. We need to remind ourselves that there are those who believe that if they reject the love of God together with the Sacrifice of His Son the Lord Jesus, their eternal future will be merely oblivion. The teaching of Scripture however is very clear and the absolute and final statement given to us is by Almighty God Himself together with His Son the Lord Jesus cannot be ignored. This can never be altered or eliminated at any future time.

(g) The final warning concerning this Book of Revelation is that there must be no additions throughout the entire book and neither must anything be removed, changed or altered in any way concerning anything that has been written in this book. The penalty for either is extremely severe, 22:18-19.

(h) The final promise that we are given is that the Lord Jesus Christ "is coming quickly" to fulfil His many promises. This great Book finishes with the promise that "The grace of the Lord Jesus Christ be with you all, Amen". 22:20-21.

L. THE ESENTIAL CHALLENGE OF THIS UNIQUE WORK THAT ALMIGHTY GOD HAS GIVEN US IS THAT IT CONTAINS FAR MORE THAN A MERE INTERESTING DISCUSSION. IT IS HIS LIVING WORD THAT GOD HAS GIVEN US.

(a) Many believe that the main teaching of the Book of Revelation is concerned with that of the Second Coming of the Lord Jesus Christ. But if we study this seriously we will discover that this is not quite as straight forward as many would believe. Because of this, there is much that sincere prayerful study will reveal to those who are willing to allow the Lord Jesus to demonstrate His will. To understand what God would teach us, we need to study sincerely what He has revealed in His Word.

(b) God's pattern in His word is very clear and obvious. The main divisions are listed leaving us in no doubt whatever. Chapter one is concerned with an important introduction.

(c) The first main division is chapters 2 to 3. This deals with the main historical era from the time of John being on the Isle of Patmos until the dramatic change in (d).

(d) The second main division is chapters 4 to 5. This is clearly set in Heaven and reveals the essential fact that the rapture will be revealed by this event.

(e) Chapter 6. The six seals upon this earth. These are the first of the terrible judgments that God pours upon those who reject His mercy.

(f) Chapter 7. This is divided into two separate but very close important teachings. The first section is concerned with the faithful tribes of Israel. The final climax is that throughout all earth there is a special time of peace while the 144,000 are sealed by the Lord. The second section is concerned with those who come out of the great tribulation.   The actual term of "the great tribulation" occurs only twice in scripture, both times in Revelation (2:22 and 7:14). The first is a severe warning emphasising the need for repentance. The second is concerned with those who have turned in true repentance during that special opportunity that God gave to those who came out of the Great Tribulation.

(g) The third main division is chapters 8 to 13. This reveals an increasing attempt of Satan and the two terrible beasts to usurp total control over all in the world.

(h) Chapters 14 and 15 now reveal some special events, a few of which will occur in Heaven, while others are upon earth. This is all leading to the clear division between those who have been faithful under extreme conditions and those who continue to defy Almighty God.

(i) Chapters 16 to 18. The final defeat of Babylon.

(j) Chapter 19. The preparing of the way for the final return of our Lord to this earth, v1-6. The marriage supper of the Lamb in Heaven, v7-10. The return of the Lord to this earth and the defeat of Satan and his armies, v11-21.

(k) Chapter 20. Satan bound for 1000 years, v1-3. 1000 years
     reign with Jesus Christ, v4-6. Rebellion by Satan and Gog
     and Magog, v7-10. The Great White Throne Judgement,
     v11-15.

(l) Chapter 21. New Heaven and new Earth.

(m) Chapter 22. The river of life, v1-5. The final warning, v6-
     17. A severe warning concerning false prophecy, v18-19.
     The final promise, v20-21.

www.ingramcontent.com/pod-product-compliance
Lightning Source LLC
Chambersburg PA
CBHW050949050726

47592CB00007B/2494